The Magic Bookshelf

This book is dedicated in memory of my father, Richard Jarvis
—R.J.

and in memory of my grandparents, Bruce and Riley Gettys
—J.J.

The Magic Bookshelf

A Parents' Guide to Showing Growing Minds the Path to
the Best Children's Literature

Janie and Richard Jarvis

First Edition

Lorica Publishing
Atlanta, Ga.

Cover Design/Illustration by Mike Butler

The Magic Bookshelf
A Parents' Guide to Showing Growing Minds the Path to the Best Children's Literature

By Janie and Richard Jarvis

Published by:

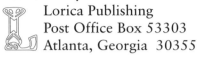 Lorica Publishing
Post Office Box 53303
Atlanta, Georgia 30355

Grateful acknowledgment is made for permission to use the following material:
pp. 32-33: Excerpt from *Tuck Everlasting* by Natalie Babbitt. Copyright 1975 by Natalie Babbitt. Reprinted by permission of Farrar, Straus & Giroux, Inc.

Publisher's Cataloging-in-Publication
(Provided by Quality Books, Inc.)

Jarvis, Janie, 1964-
    The magic bookshelf : a parents' guide to showing growing minds the path to the best children's literature / Janie and Richard Jarvis ; cover design/illustration by Mike Butler. -- 1st ed.
    p. cm.
    Includes bibliographical references and index.
    LCCN: 98-96291
    ISBN: 0-9665111-0-7

    1. Reading--Parent participation. 2. Children--Books and reading. 3. Children's literature--Bibliography. I. Jarvis, Richard, 1962- II. Title.

LB1050.J37 1999   372.4
                                 QBI98-1670

The child who is exposed, naturally, as a normal part of a happy home life, to the best work of good writers, is fortunate indeed. And the best way to achieve this is of course to give him books which have been chosen with care ...
— *Frank Eyre, from* British Children's Books in the Twentieth Century

There is so much to teach and time goes so fast.
— *Erma Bombeck*

About the Authors

Janie and Richard Jarvis are journalists and parents who make their home in Atlanta, Georgia.

Janie has been a reporter for newspapers including *The Greenville (SC) News* and *The Atlanta Journal-Constitution*. Her work also has appeared in various national magazines. She works from home as a speech and correspondence writer for the Atlanta diplomatic office of the Republic of China on Taiwan. Janie's lifelong study of children's literature includes courses at Emory University in Atlanta on juvenile literature and writing.

Richard's journalism experience includes five years as the education reporter for *The Greenville Piedmont*, an afternoon newspaper. He later worked as assistant city editor for *The Greenville News*, and is executive editor for an Atlanta-based publisher of newsletters for tax and human resources professionals.

Both are graduates of the University of South Carolina in Columbia; Richard *cum laude* with degrees in history and journalism, and Janie with a degree in English with a writing concentration.

The Jarvises have two boys: Allen, 10, from Richard's first marriage; and Riley, 1.

Table of Contents

vii

Acknowledgments

We would like to thank the following people and organizations for their kind and invaluable assistance in writing this book:

Lucia Raatma for her personal evaluation of our manuscript; Russ Underwood for proofreading the manuscript; the Atlanta-Fulton Public Library, particularly for its on-line title research, book holding system, and Information Line, and the Ida B. Williams (Buckhead) branch for its hands-on research aids and personal staff assistance; Joel Patrick for his book publishing expertise and helpful tips; Dan Poynter for his book publishing aids and information; Marilyn and Tom Ross for the book publishing advice in their book; Mary Patrick and Debbie Strickland for their personal chapter critiques and other valuable input; the Banquet Bible Study members for their prayers and support; Kathleen Courtney for her support and encouragement in this book's earliest stages; Martin Kahn of the Service Corps of Retired Executives Association for his early business advice; Carol Lee Lorenzo for two and a half years' worth of children's writing instruction and for her discriminating taste in children's literature; Janet Conley for her book list suggestions; Amazon.com for its vast database and inventory, and quick delivery of our research tools; Regina Lovette, Edith Jarvis, Susan Hasty, Robin Hall, and all our other friends for their moral support; and last, but not least, Allen and Riley Jarvis and John Helsel for their concrete examples of the joy books can bring children.

Manifesto for a Reader

The Roman poet Cicero called books "the food of youth." But let's face it. Many of us operate on the "good enough" philosophy when it comes to our children's reading. How many times have you heard peers say: "Well, at least he's reading something ..." when they talk about a lack of interest in reading beyond comic books and pulpy stuff?

Look at it this way. Would you say: "At least she's eating something ..." if your child would only touch candy bars and soda pop? Of course not. Why, then, do many parents forget that brains, like bodies, need developing with nourishment and exercise?

Everything we know about early learning and development points to the need to provide rich experiences for children if they are to mature into thoughtful and purposeful adults. According to Dorothy Butler's research in *Babies Need Books,* about one half of a person's intelligence quotient is developed by age four, with the next thirty percent accruing by the age of eight. The more meaningful experiences children are exposed to, the better and faster their brains develop. We know that children who lack this fullness of experience often develop more slowly and fall a step behind their more culturally advantaged peers. Sadly, a child who doesn't use his brain at age ten is unlikely to get much use out of it as an adult.

Contrary to what many like to believe, intellectual achievement is not a function of income. Most families have access to a public library or bookmobile, and most can tune in a radio station that broadcasts classical and other cultural music. Just as research indicates children who listen to Mozart at a young age have quicker mental development, even more research shows that young children who are exposed early to excellent books and literature will do better throughout their educational career, and consequently become more empowered as adults. Now, as neither radio nor books are hobbies that require much money to sustain them, this is quite affordable supplementary education indeed.

Yet a common reaction to suggestions that children read (or be read) better written, more challenging literature than just the popular "lowest common denominator" fare is, "Oh, just let them be kids and read kid stuff. They're only children once." Exactly! That's why, though such a reaction sounds kindly at first blush, that same parent (or even educator) might as well say, "They're only children. They don't need or deserve to read anything really *good.*"

We suspect adults with this mentality have somehow developed distorted impressions of what it means to encourage the reading of good books. For one, many fail to understand what a good book is. They envision themselves yanking away a child's prized horror book and solemnly replacing it with some dusty, impossibly boring tome, with the dubious reassurance, "This is good for you. You might not realize it now, but you'll thank me later."

Now, that *is* grim! But as silly—and scary—as that scenario might seem, it does somewhat accurately describe what some of us, in our quick-fix computer age, have come to think. However, the approach we encourage doesn't call for feeding books to children like some literary spinach. We're not talking about morality tales written in antiquated prose, or advanced classics that are tedious and difficult to understand. Anyone familiar with Dr. Seuss knows a thought-provoking book doesn't have to be hard to read and appreciate. In fact, it's quite the opposite.

This book aims to show parents how to create more literate environments for their children, regardless of age or reading level, and to guide them to books that can truly make a difference in their children's lives. This environment will include your own "literary legacies" and the finest children's classics, which will open the door to a lifetime of cultural literacy. But most of all, you and your family will find a core of worthwhile, high quality books—both modern and older—that might not be familiar to you now but are so good that captivated young readers will be unable to put them down. For this is the true great "kid's stuff."

As well as entertaining children and telling stories strong enough to live in their memories for years to come, good books can teach them how to deal with challenging circumstances and demonstrate how life presents actions and consequences. In today's world, we are judged by our ability to solve problems. Through literary works like *My Side of the Mountain* by Jean Craighead George and *Tuck Everlasting* by Natalie Babbitt, which happen to be books with radically different themes, children can learn to become "outside the box" thinkers. Many adults have even said that in their own childhoods, books seemed to have been their main support systems in difficult times.

Our philosophy is one of opportunity, not deprivation. We shouldn't let high-tech, but limited, pursuits and subliterature steal our children's brief moments of availability for books that can help lay the foundation for entire lifetimes of innovative thinking and learning. Picasso asserted that children are artistic because they haven't learned to clamp down on their imaginations like adults. Childhood is but a brief season in life. As parents, we are obligated to nurture the creativity and innocence while it's at its peak.

Research conducted with children from Eastern European orphanages shows us that lost time is hard—perhaps impossible—to make up. Dr. Seuss, E.B. White, Katherine Paterson, Lloyd Alexander, and other fine authors have only a moment available to reach inside those darkened rooms of the mind and find the light switch. Your child's future asks that you give proven experts like these a chance to make magic.

The beauty of this is, aside from the obvious gradual benefits of growing up in a reading culture, good books introduce vivid imaginary worlds of joyful escape, and instruct children in ways that are important to them, thus enriching their imaginations and even the quality of their outside lives *now*. How can we improve on that?

Janie and Richard Jarvis
Atlanta, Georgia

I am well aware not only of the importance of children—whom we naturally cherish and who also embody our hopes for the future— but also of the importance of what we provide for them in the way of art; and I realize that we are competing with a lot of cultural influences, some of which beguile them in false directions.
—William Steig, Caldecott-winning author/illustrator of Sylvester and the Magic Pebble *and* Doctor De Soto

The Magic Bookshelf

Books are magical. They comfort us when we feel sad, uplift us in times of joy, and transport us to other times and places. We feel this magic as adults. But for children, the magic is much stronger. Young imaginations skip easily from reality to fantasy, and live safely in both worlds. And books can move your children through the transitions and phases of life unlike anything else.

In this book we talk about a "Magic Bookshelf," which is both a literal and fanciful concept that springs from our philosophy on reading and the literature of childhood. Childhood is a fleeting genie—once it escapes the bottle, it's gone. When high school comes, your children will not go back and read the juvenile classics that could otherwise have enriched their lifetimes. Quite simply, childhood is too brief to be squandered on reading material that doesn't challenge and engage the mind and imagination.

In a concrete sense, a Magic Bookshelf consists of the good books you encounter—the ones you own, those read to you, and those you borrow from libraries and friends. But in a larger sense, a Magic Bookshelf exists in the mind: it's the collection of rich stories, characters, and ideas that remains with you long after the books have been read, that becomes a part of you, that continues to delight and influence you for the rest of your days. Consider the anecdote about the elderly man who reflects on the many interesting people he's met during his life. Then it dawns on him that half of them were characters from books.

A Magic Bookshelf can become a fixture in any household. It's never too soon, or too late, to build it. In fact, you may already have the beginnings of one in your house. Perhaps you've saved some treasured books from your childhood; maybe your child has already received some special books as gifts. It could be you've picked up a few promising-looking books with well-turned pages at a recent garage sale, or attractive overstocks at a local bookstore.

But chances are these would-be good friends mostly sit neglected, crowded out by faddish series books, videos, flashy CD-ROMs, and the cable guide.

The truth is, there are thousands of well-written, thoughtfully conceived books with richly textured plots and characters, for your child to read and enjoy, and be positively influenced by. The problem is, how do you lead your child to them? How do you even find these "good books" amid the mass-marketing bells and whistles attached to the glossy new children's books in the stores? Where's the truly "good stuff" and how can we get our hands on it? Besides, how can books compete with the many distractions and complications of modern life, when many children don't even make it home until they get out of their after-school or sports programs, or other lessons, and the like?

Our Magic Bookshelf came to be when we started trying to find challenging and interesting books to introduce to Allen, Richard's son from his first marriage, who was then eight years old. The roots of this mission sprang from our own childhoods. Janie had even held on to favorite books from her elementary and middle school years, with their lovingly worn pages, memorized plot lines, and familiar drawings—*The Chronicles of Narnia, The Secret Garden,* and dozens of others. Janie's stepfather, a rare book dealer, had contributed significantly to this collection with first edition classics.

We later started referring to the shelf that contained this highly valued book collection as the Magic Bookshelf because every book we pulled out for Allen to read seemed to be a hit. And it gave way to a whole new way of seeing books.

Before this phenomenon, outgoing, city-bred Allen favored athletics and math, but had developed good listening skills by having been read aloud to since babyhood (see Book-Lovers from Babyhood, p. 45). Allen's competitive nature also made him eager to learn to read in school, to keep up. But he wasn't the natural reader we seemed to have been in childhood.

When he'd go to the library with us, or visit his school library, he'd try to give out-of-class reading a stab. He'd check out a big stack of Goosebumps books that he would dutifully begin to read. But he never finished them. We think he read the first two chapters of every Goosebumps book published. But he never finished them ... .

One day Janie retrieved her copy of Roald Dahl's *Charlie and the Chocolate Factory* from the "Magic Bookshelf." Unsure if Allen could read this comparatively challenging book for himself, Richard began reading it to him at night when Allen came over for his regular visits. (You don't even have to see your child every day to make this work. See If Your Child Does Not Live With You, p. 81). Each night he was with us, we'd read more of this wonderful book. We even spent some sunny Saturday afternoons indoors reading and laughing out loud at the story and its marvelous, witty images—golden tickets, Square Candies that Look 'Round, Everlasting Gobstoppers, a chocolate river ... .

But here's the real magic. Allen soon went to the library and checked out more Roald Dahl books to read for himself. These and other books we thought were above his reading level were read start to finish within days. Without his realizing it, hours would go by, during which he would occasionally look up and proudly say, "I've read one hundred more pages." Allowance dollars that were once spent on candy and toys were soon actually being saved up to buy books as well. Often he would buy a book he'd already read because he wanted to own it and read it again at his leisure. He still kept up with his old favorite pursuits—soccer, science activities, hanging around with friends—but the reading seemed to add a new dimension to his personality and his life. It became part of his identity, and it stuck.

Even car trips have become a whole new experience. Long

treks to see grandparents melt away as the pages turn. We often have to remain in the car for a few extra minutes as Allen begs for a few minutes to finish a page or chapter. Once, upon returning home late at night, he woke up and said, "Please, let me just finish this chapter." Books had even seeped into his dreams.

We believe this can be so for many other children. They just need to find, or be shown, the path to the books that will engage them.

Why "Good" Books?

Many of us grew up on comic books, Nancy Drew and Hardy Boys mysteries, and other popular fare. If that is true, and modern substitutes are so easily found (an understatement if you've noted the legions of series books on the market these days), why should you worry about whether your children read the "good stuff?" Aren't they better off mastering the latest computer learning programs and watching "educational TV?" Isn't the future in technology anyway? The answer is no, not in a substantial sense, and particularly not when it comes to succeeding in school and getting into college.

Look at your state's universities and check out their average SAT scores. While the newspapers bemoan the fact that test scores are sinking, college administrators have a different story to tell. Many lower achieving students choose trade schools and community colleges, but even formerly less competitive state-supported schools are reporting their freshmen arrive bearing better entrance scores and high school grades than ever before. And the best school in your state may well be turning away applicants who would have made it in easily a decade ago. In addition, most people can forget out-of-state schools. To better serve students who live in state, some schools are raising out-of-state tuition by as much as ten percent a year.

Is your child ready to compete in this new, competitive world? Are you sure she has the tools it will take to make it?

Reading, and particularly reading high-quality literature, is a proven way to give your child a better shot at competing, by unharnessing his imagination, offering him new confidence that comes with broadened experience, and helping him acquire the grammar and spelling skills necessary to survive middle school, not to mention giving him stories that will stay in his heart for the rest of his life.

We're not talking about just the classic books, or only the ones that have been judged best by panels of adult critics, or dry-as-dust "read this because it's good for you" fare. We mean well-written—that is not to say hard to read—books with fantastic stories that send children to new worlds full of fresh concepts, or which introduce captivating characters who face challenges and situations readers may or may not be facing themselves. We mean books that have been warmly embraced by all kinds of modern children, but which, because of their flashily displayed, "quick fix" competition, more often sit in shadows on the bookstore shelves.

Parents sometimes attribute their children's resistance to reading good books to a mere preference for the pulp. "I want them to like to read," they say. "Those other books bore them. I don't want to spoil their already fragile interest." There's one main reason why competent readers eschew better quality books for mass-market products. It's the same reason children prefer TV. It's easier. It requires hardly any thought. And it's human nature to prefer to coast. But we all know this world requires too much of one's wits to effectively live that way.

The problem of children neglecting more challenging books virtually can be avoided with a reading lifestyle that starts them off very young. For older children, it's a bit trickier. We should never tell children the subliterature they're reading is "trash"— even if we think it is. This would, of course, trigger negative attitudes toward the activity in general, and perhaps seriously wound their pride. Too, such abject disapproval may well drive them in the opposite direction. As children's author Katherine Paterson cautions in her book *Gates of Excellence: On Reading and Writing Books for Children*: "If we prescribe books as medicine, our children have a perfect right to refuse the nasty-tasting spoon." The way to approach such a situation is to find—or best, help your child "happen upon"—better substitutes. (See Good Taste is Learned, p. 31.)

Unfortunately, many children picture an adult's idea of "better" as bearing golden seal stickers, or having crowds of teachers and librarians whistling and applauding behind this superior object. We've got to prove to children a book is better because it offers a better subject, a better story, better characters, and better ideas to think about.

It's a cop-out to say, "She should read what she wants. I don't want to force it." You don't have to force. What you do have to do is prove to your child that there are finer books out there that she will enjoy just as much, maybe more. Sure, she can keep up her comic book collection. But how will she know there's anything else?

It's critical to note a child doesn't have to be college-bound or among the brightest in his class to benefit greatly from reading good literature. In fact, this truth about better books holds just as firmly when a child is at the *bottom* of the class. Good books are written for all children. Good books help a child be the best *he* can be. But though your child certainly doesn't have to know it, this too is urgent business—childhood is fleeting. Just think of yourself—how long did your childhood seem to last?

This guide aims to give parents suggestions as to how to offer the invaluable tools reading can give your child. We aren't talking about teaching children how to read in general, or even just how to interest them in reading for the sake of it. We're talking about teaching children *to read on higher content levels, to read good books.*

The Book Scene Today

Most of us grew up in at least slightly simpler times. The personal computer explosion, the Internet, and even cable television caught hold after many of us were well into college or already on our own. There seemed not to be quite so much competition for our time.

Yet our culture is still very book-oriented, and library traffic remains high. The book industry appears to be thriving, and children's books are especially hot. According to publishing experts at R.R. Bowker's, there are currently more than 127,000 children's books in print! And that figure doesn't include the scads of out-of-print, perennially popular books that still line library shelves. Compare this with the 35,000 books in print in the early 1970s. (Even then, books like *Down the Rabbit Hole: Adventures and Misadventures in the Realm of Children's Literature* by Selma G. Lanes were being written to help parents navigate the children's book maze.) The bookstores continue to be glutted with new additions to their collections.

But there's a difference between what's big business and what's worth the money. Fortunately there are some very good books being published today. There are also many painfully mediocre books being published—and bought—as well. Publishers, who are mostly interested in sales and merchandising, will rarely introduce something new and innovative, in favor of reissuing older books in cheap new editions, or imitating what has been popular before, adhering to the formula.

Publishers are usually looking for the sure sell. Books by big names and celebrities, like former British Royal Family member Sarah Ferguson, comedian and actor Bill Cosby, and movie actress Jamie Lee Curtis, are rushed into print. Only occasionally is an unknown writer lucky enough to be "discovered" by an open-minded and determined editor.

Meanwhile, book merchandising is rampant. For example, the "concept" series Sweet Valley High is one of the hottest sellers for pre-teenage girls today. (We don't mean to target this series; there are plenty of others, such as the spun sugar spin-offs of characters plucked from hit TV series.) Written by a host of different authors whose chief requirement is to generate quick copy, these books are of inferior quality but sell by the boatload. Cheap ancillary products like diaries, novelty book-of-the-month clubs, videos and TV shows fuel the marketing frenzy. The creators make a killing. But is reading these books doing any more for young people than easily passing the time or offering a juvenile version of "guilty pleasure" reading? Are there really any clever ideas or intriguing characters introduced in them? (And would we want our children to emulate these one-dimensional characters like the plastic-perfect Sweet Valley twins and their phony friends anyway?)

There definitely is a place, and a need, for escape reading. We all enjoy our "beach blanket" books, and giving our brains a break. In our own youths most of us probably breezed through many a quickie book based on some movie, or comic books, or dime-a-dozen mystery novels. It's not our intention to put down all the current trendy books. Actually, some, like The Boxcar Children, started out as captivating stories spun by one talented writer. But with many protracted series (we're not talking about the books that naturally give way to a sequel or two), when the merchandising steps in and the original writer can no longer keep up with the demand—from the publisher as much as the readers—the books are farmed out, their quality is diluted, and the books become shells of the original work. They become mere products.

Meanwhile, there are so many good books that could quite possibly mean a great deal to your children, and even stick in the backs of their minds for the rest of their lives—if they were read. Many parents, writers of magazine articles, and even educators make the claim that, "any reading is good reading." We, however, believe that allowing children to always choose sub-par reading material will deny them the opportunity to experience the real magic reading can offer.

This book was written to help parents and other guardians guide children to literature that is truly special, in a natural and non-didactic way. In back, you'll find a comprehensive book list. (It is by no means is a definitive list, but it suggests books that are beloved by children, as well as recommended by literary experts, other parents, and ourselves.) Once on the right path, your children will learn to make wonderful choices for themselves.

In the end, we hope that everyone can experience the great joy and lifelong benefits of having their own personal Magic Bookshelves—both material and of the mind.

Train a child in the way that he should go, and when he is old he will not turn from it.

—Proverbs 22:6

Do As I Do

Who is the biggest influence on how devoted a reader your child becomes? Teachers? The local librarians and bookstore clerks? No, the answer is *you*. As a parent (or grandparent or guardian), you are the most important person in your child's life. You're also the strongest example he looks to when choosing favorite activities.

Think about how your children copy your behavior. Have you ever watched a boy practice "shaving" in front of a mirror with his dad? How about a little girl sitting at a computer and tapping away at the keys, pretending to be working like her mother?

Reading is no different. Children who grow up in non-reading households are likely to be non-readers. And if you ask children to read classic-quality literature while your coffee table is stacked high with tabloids and the TV is always on, why should they take your advice? Remember, you represent what your children want to be. Shouldn't you begin with the strong example of making reading good books a central activity in your home?

A certain status is attached to the act of reading when a child constantly sees her parents choosing reading over other activities, and hears them discussing books and other reading material. When a child is born into such a family, these standards are automatically set. Children don't always mind their parents or appear to respect the family standards, of course. But it's a fact that living standards and lifestyles are learned and copied, and incorporated into the child's behavior and "worldview." He thinks, "This is what my family does."

Research continually pounds home the message that you can't start reading aloud to a child too early. Studies have shown that the sooner parents begin reading to children—from birth is not too early—the higher the child's reading level will be upon entering school. (See Book-Lovers From Babyhood, p. 45.)

Although some children do learn to read at home, most are taught the mechanics of reading by educators, beginning in kindergarten or first grade. Good teachers can help children get comfortable with books and develop a healthy respect for reading through reading aloud, introducing reading-oriented projects, and stocking their classroom shelves well. Allen's imaginative second-grade teacher assigned her students to write and illustrate their own books, complete with dedications and blurbs about the author. Then the class held an author's day for parents. Parents "met the authors" and enjoyed refreshments after all the children read their books aloud.

Naturally, this attaches importance to literature and books. Children believe what they do is special when such a fuss is made. Imagine the status reading gains through activities like this!

However, the parent's role is essential. Apart from the children who are naturally inspired by books from an early age, most teachers can't instill a love for reading or promote reading as a lifestyle. They just don't have time. Their days with the children end at about two o'clock in the afternoon. Besides, during the school day, teachers must cover a myriad of other subjects and requirements.

Some time back, teachers could afford to devote part of a school day to "quiet reading time." Now, teachers often are compelled to add to their curriculum classes such as computer literacy and drug awareness, which may be beneficial but still encroach on the classroom downtime teachers once had. Researchers who set out to find what students did with their average school days found that children spend two hours a day on worksheets and other exercises, and a mere twelve minutes actually reading books.

How often do you hear educators talk about trying to find a way to "get children reading?" A constantly stressed curriculum is too crowded to find room for something so simple as reading for pleasure. The likelihood of children doing sufficient reading during the school day is slim. (Also consider the unfortunate buzzword used in some schools to refer to reading a book aloud: "reading event." If it must be called an "event," it probably doesn't happen too often, does it? And teachers who are obliged to plan such "reading events" probably don't have a prayer of introducing other reading time into the classroom, as much as they might like to.)

If you believe your child reads enough at school, this is likely not so. According to Judi Paul, developer of The Accelerated Reader, a computer program for school use, the time allotted for actual reading in the classroom dwindles from that scant twelve minutes a day for fourth graders to almost nothing for older students. Parents who belong to strong PTA's might consider asking their child's school for a curriculum improvement that more heavily emphasizes reading during the school day. But even the best schools have serious limitations.

At bottom, teachers can get children started, and sometimes even convince a child reading can be fun as well as educational. But it's up to you to keep the momentum going, to build on and expand the learning experience children receive at school. Even the most expensive and prestigious private schools can't accomplish this goal for you. And without this guidance, by college time it's too late. The best colleges already demand a rock-solid language background. It used to be a lack of strong reading and communication skills would put young people behind their college peers and cause them to struggle in classes that require heavy reading and writing (which is most college classes. See The Bond Between Reading and Writing, p. 51). Now, those without superior language skills don't even get into these same colleges.

In *The Read-Aloud Handbook*, Jim Trelease claims that in homes where reading and other forms of communication aren't encouraged, a child will enter school markedly deprived of the

All parents should ask themselves constantly, "What have we given our children?" "What effort have we made to pass on to them the culture that we inherited and to help them to go a step further and become more aware than we were of what art, literature and music can give us?"
— Frank Eyre, from British Children's Books in the Twentieth Century

Leaving Your Own Literary Legacy: Incorporate Your Own 'Literary Heritage' into Your Child's Magic Bookshelf

If you still have some old, cherished books from childhood, or re-member some standard library favorites, by all means pull them out, try to wheedle them away from your parents, or order them from an out-of-print catalog if they're hard to find. Take the time to re-read and reflect on these books you loved so much as a child—even if they some-times seem far from "fine literature." This is a concept apart from try-ing to always read the "best stuff." This is passing along pieces of your own literary heritage to your children.

If you loved a certain gift book written in so-so verse as a child, or a favorite relative gave you a now-treasured Little Golden Book and inscribed it, then it should be shared with your children. This will prob-ably go for most all the books you saved from your childhood (or else you wouldn't have saved them).

And while some of the books we save could be considerably less than classics, others are sure to be. Classics get that name because nobody throws them away. How many women still have well-worn copies of *Little Women* on their bookshelves? And how many of your parents have boxes of Dr. Seuss books stored in their attics? Your own legacy may be better than you at first think, and it certainly represents an unusual opportunity to create bonds across generations when you share your favorites with your children.

What you're doing is making a literary legacy of your childhood book collection. And that's another function of books: they provide highly personal, priceless experiences you can share. This is why, though adults sometimes are tempted to unload adult books they'll never read again, in general it's not good to get rid of a children's book (unless you truly don't care for it, or you or other children found it scary or other-wise objectionable). Children's books are commodities. Once a person becomes an adult, few items are as evocative of childhood as these distantly familiar books. And what could be more special in a child's eyes than possessing a book that was loved by his parents when they were children? Indeed, many children forget their parents *were* ever children.

Again, remember childhood passes quickly. It's important to fill those early years with rich literary experiences. Books are memories. Throughout your life, you will reflect on favorite children's books. When you later pick them up, they'll evoke nostalgia. The characters leap out as long-lost friends who are always there when you return to their timeless, fictional world.

A book reviewer for the California-based children's book catalog Chinaberry loved the little book *Mudpies and Other Recipes: A Cookbook for Dolls* by Marjorie Winslow so much as a child that she kept it all her life. Once her children were old enough to enjoy it, however, the book was so worn it was falling apart. Although the editor lucked out in finding a used copy in better condition at a bookstore, she was dismayed the book itself had fallen out of print. The Chinaberry editors were unable to persuade the first publisher to reprint it, which would have been a brick wall for some; but instead, the editors decided to take up the cause of saving this singular literary legacy by teaming with a small publisher and reprinting it themselves as a Chinaberry Classic.

Books can mold entire lives. The late Christian scholar, theologian, and beloved children's author C.S. Lewis constantly alludes to his extraordinarily rich literary heritage in many of his written works. It was books—such as *Squirrel Nutkin*, written by one of Lewis' favorite childhood authors, Beatrix Potter—that helped evoke some of his first experiences with a profound but elusive emotion, a deep yearning he called "Joy." In his book *Surprised By Joy: The Shape of My Early Life*, Lewis documented the unbreakable literary link between his early childhood and adulthood: "Many of the books that pleased me as a child, please me still," he noted. Many of us agree with Lewis' sentiment when we re-open *The Cat in the Hat*.

You needn't worry about your literary legacies looking pretty. Books that live through years of love and frequent perusal are properly worn and coming unhinged. But these books, and even paperbacks, can survive for a surprisingly long time with a little tape and glue. Jim Trelease's *Read-Aloud Handbook* includes instructions on how to extend the lives of softbacks with clear plastic shelf paper.

In sum, people should keep their personal juvenile libraries alive long after they've grown up. Bear this in mind with the books your own children acquire as well. There will be other children behind them.

basic tools she needs. She will ask fewer questions, have a smaller vocabulary, use briefer sentences, and have a shorter attention span than her more advanced peers.

A Child's Reading Identity

As parents, we also warn against classifying a child as "an athlete" or "a bookworm" or "a math wizard." Robert Fulghum notes young children are wonderfully diverse. In *All I Really Need to Know I Learned in Kindergarten*, Fulghum reminds us that five- and six-year-olds live in worlds without limits. Ask them if they can dance, and they leap up to show you. Ask them to sing, and they belt out a tune. Ask them to read, and they get out a book and read it to you. You must strive to keep this spirit of "can do" alive in your children, especially when it comes to reading. Don't agree when they say they "aren't good at that." This is more true than ever with reading. No child should believe he isn't a good reader. Remember, children believe you when you tell them who they are.

Educator and literacy expert Lucy Calkins demonstrates in her book *Raising Lifelong Learners: A Parent's Guide* how parents should use lots of vocal encouragement to reinforce children's identities as readers. Calkins suggests parents enthusiastically ask their children what's happening in their books, and otherwise introduce impromptu discussions to show their personal interest and admiration for their children's literary accomplishments.

Sure, children will have their own interests and strengths. Your child may be a great budding athlete. Play to that strength by choosing some books that have heroes who play sports, like *Maniac Magee* by Jerry Spinelli. There are also lots of good biographies available about sports figures. Imagine how inspiring books about Native American Olympic star Jim Thorpe or baseball great Lou Gehrig could be when you want to teach a child about adversity and triumph of the spirit. Or introduce a young girl to the sickly child named Wilma Rudolph, who went on to wow the world and win the Olympic gold medal for track and field. And when you light the spark by playing to your child's interest, it will be easier to introduce even more books that gradually broaden her young mind.

There is more available than ever before to please children with varied interests. There are books, both nonfiction and fiction, about horses, art, mythology, sports, even words and numbers (like the middle-grade fantasy novel *The Phantom Tollbooth* by Norton Juster). Lewis Carroll's *Through the Looking Glass* is plotted as a giant chess game. This is not to suggest that you have to turn a physical, or extremely gregarious, child into one who will be willing to constantly sit still and read. But you can encourage him to be a regular reader by making your book choices and purchases stand out for him.

Books about children's particular areas of interest can not only boost their knowledge of the subject, but improve their confidence and help validate and define their identities, by giving them a sense of expertise. With the already dedicated readers too, it's important to recognize special interests and nurture them with books.

Once again, your example is critical. Show children how you use books to learn and grow in your own life. Do you read about history? Let your child know. Maybe you can pick a topic to research together. Do you have a presentation to give or perhaps a Sunday School lesson to teach? Go to the library and take your child along to show her the process. Show her that reading is power. Give her a strong example of how that power is used.

In summary, reading is a lifestyle. Parents and other guardians are the only people who can make this so. The best way to achieve this reality is to initiate reading as early as infancy—and if not then, as soon as the child begins to study the behaviors around him and practice them, and take them into his heart as the way life is.

There's Still Time to Change

Parents shouldn't think they've totally missed the boat if their families arrive later on the reading scene. Perhaps you and your spouse have always enjoyed other activities more than reading and browsing in bookstores and libraries. Non-readers often consider reading a solitary—meaning lonely—activity. As a regular reader will attest, this isn't true, not when you have wonderful characters to keep you company and adventures to fill your mind.

Further, many people don't realize you don't have to always be alone, or even quiet, when reading. You can listen to books on tape in the car, and read aloud while waiting in the doctor's office, sitting around a campfire, or giving the children's nighttime bath. A story in *Harper's Bazaar* magazine chronicled the life of a personal shopper at the designer house Prada, whose way of winding down after a hectic day was taking a book to a jazz club.

Always keep in mind that though children might not see you reading while riding public transportation to work, for example, your discussing the book with your spouse or your children that evening is also a part of this reading lifestyle.

In most of this guide we advocate reading as a behavior, an activity that is simply accepted and practiced and lived by the family. You can start any time, just as you have whenever you've introduced any other new regimen or practice in your household, such as eating more healthily, attending religious services more regularly, or buying a family computer. Books and reading are some of the most important benefits—and farthest-reaching ones—you can offer your family.

My father bought all the books he read and never got rid of any of them. There were books in the study, books in the drawing room, books in the cloakroom, books (two deep) in the great bookcase on the landing, books in a bedroom, books piled as high as my shoulder in the cistern attic, books of all kinds reflecting every transient stage of my parents' interest, books readable and unreadable, books suitable for a child and books most emphatically not ... .
—C. S. Lewis, *from* Surprised by Joy: The Shape of My Early Life

Nurturing the Reading Habit, Naturally

The way to acquaint a child with books, and to nurture the love of them, is to have the child live with them, among them, in them. For reading to be natural, books must not only be enthusiastically encouraged by adults, but books must simply be always accessible to the child. That means, they must literally be everywhere.

This isn't hard to do. Other chapters in this book discuss how to acquire great books, even on the slimmest of budgets. Pulling out these gems and displaying them as an integral part of the home—not only in the child's room—is your next step.

Likewise, there are many ways to incorporate reading into the flow of energy in your home, into your family's and child's routine. Here are some ideas to consider in getting started.

How to Encourage Reading in the Home and Out

◆ Books should be highly visible in your home. Make them furniture. They should be shelved or propped in accessible places like coffee and end tables, bedside tables, shelves in bunk beds, and so on. Place books you want children to handle on easy-to-reach shelves and surfaces, and store the nicer books up high where they'll stay safe.

Encourage this natural contact with books so they are considered regular parts of children's lives, not just objects to be admired from afar or brought out on special occasions (except for the truly valuable books you might acquire).

If you're just starting on a "permanent" home library, consider the boxes and boxes of books—dog-eared assigned paperbacks from high school and college, nice hardbacks, or textbooks you still value—that were stashed away for lack of a place to put them. These forgotten books can serve as the beginning of making books a stronger presence in your home. Invest in some good shelving if possible—though clever makeshift shelving works just as well—and bring those old books out of exile to display in family rooms, if not the living and dining rooms. Again, these don't all have to be children's books. Your goal is to set an example.

To flesh out your collection, join book clubs or visit secondhand bookstores to find nice-looking but inexpensive hardbacks. Also, watch for bargains on the discount tables at most bookstores. You can often find nice editions of classic books for sale at one-fourth their original prices. The point is to think of books as being as critical to your rooms as furniture, and get everybody comfortable having them around.

Childhood reading expert Dorothy Butler suggests that parents—especially those uncomfortable with books as toys for young children—think of books as nourishment, food for developing minds. Also, just as children need to learn to eat with the proper utensils, so too must they learn how to handle and properly read a book. This takes some initial bumbling. Later, you'll teach your children how to care for their books. But for now, designate some books for practice. Aside from the usual sturdy children's volumes, obsolete textbooks and other out-of-date tomes can serve to help your child through these often awkward first steps at page turning and other book handling skills.

◆ Equip your child's room with proper reading lights at bedside, and perhaps by a favorite comfortable chair. Do the same in the family room. In *Raising Lifelong Learners*, Lucy Calkins describes how her children made comfortable reading nests. With pillows, blankets, and nearby heaters, they got cozy and helped themselves to the baskets of books beside them.

Calkins also details how, as her children grew older, she converted naptimes to reading times. Given the choice between napping and reading, they'd choose reading and feel privileged. Likewise, Calkins allows her children thirty to forty-five minutes of reading time before lights-out, another way to make them feel they've earned a grown-up privilege.

◆ In the chapter Do As I Do (p. 9), we discussed how parents should read more themselves if they're not already avid readers. The most well-intentioned of reading programs will fail if parents don't read. Incorporate books into your own life, so children will see you reading and enjoying books and other printed material. Young, impressionable children really do think what you do is admirable, and want to copy you.

Openly discuss books with your spouse and children. When children read, show your personal interest by enthusiastically inquiring about what's happening in the book. And stick around for an answer. Offer high praise for their reading efforts. As Lucy Calkins suggests, praising a child for being a good reader is both reward for the effort he's made and a self-fulfilling prophesy. Why do we find it so easy to cheer loudly when our children do well in sports, yet we never seem to able to offer remotely the same encouragement for exercising mental abilities?

So, remember to look over your child's shoulder every now and again. Books are considered great discussion topics among adults, yet we forget to do the same with our children. The themes of many of the books listed in the appendix can give you the opportunity to have truly meaningful conversations with your children. After all, you have some life lessons to share, and your children may be waiting for you to open the door.

However, for any of these strategies to be effective, you must avoid treating reading as an assignment situation by always insinuating "there will be a discussion afterward," or getting between the child and the book too much. Likewise, you must not make reading an isolating activity. Either approach will be regarded as punishment, or just as bad, homework. In their March/April 1997 *Horn Book Magazine* article "Have Book Bag, Will

Travel: Reading Aloud," Mary M. Burns and Ann A. Flowers say it well: "Story hour is not simply school in disguise." Reading should not be a solemn activity. It has to be fun. For that to be, reading must be natural.

◆ Don't spare "book gifts." If you are browsing in a store and spot an inexpensive softback that looks promising, buy it if your budget permits, even if you would be unwilling to spend the same five dollars at a toy store. Teach your child that a book is a desirable present or surprise.

When you turn the buying of a book into a special event or treat, you're more than halfway there in teaching children the value of books. This in turn will make them feel important for receiving a book, as well as for reading it.

While you're at it, don't forget to indulge in the trappings of a true reader. Buy affordable but important-looking stick-on name-plates for your child's own books, as well as whimsical and fancy (looking) bookmarks, to convey and affirm a sense of ownership. A set of fun bookends would also make a special gift.

◆ Regard your childrens' books as their private property. Don't ever throw them out or give them away without their permission. (Children don't have very good judgment about this sometimes, anyway. In their later years they might sorely regret having traded away their childhood book collection. See Leaving Your Own Literary Legacy, p. 12.)

Every child should have his own library, no matter how small. Money is not even always required to get books—schools have programs like RIF (Reading Is FUNdamental), where free books are regularly issued. And most children eventually have some pocket change for their own personal spending. Encourage them to buy books with their own money. This, as just mentioned, leads them to regard books as desirable possessions.

◆ Try to gain tighter control over TV viewing in your home. TV is a passive, not interactive, activity. It discourages analysis by offering only a one-dimensional view of life, in both picture and content. (See How to Wean a TV Junkie—Or Avoid the Habit Altogether, p. 27.)

It's not necessary to toss the TV out the window, of course. But like other things you want a child to experience in small doses only, you've got to get a handle on it. TV can be an enormous time-waster. You might consider taping several shows the child enjoys, like *Arthur*, *The Magic Schoolbus*, or *Wishbone*, and reserving small blocks of time for watching those and other programs. But whenever you realize the TV is serving merely as background noise, unplug it and substitute nice music and quiet conversation—or family reading time.

◆ Encourage writing in the home, from the dutiful writing of correspondence such as thank-you letters to e-mail, if your household is into computers; and journal-keeping on a computer or in spiral-bound diaries. (See The Bond Between Reading and Writing, p. 51.) The syndicated modern etiquette columnist Miss Manners believes children are never too young to compose their own thank-yous, even if the sentiments of very young children have to be transcribed by a parent or an older child. As well as learning the art of being properly gracious, this bread-and-butter note writing serves to familiarize your child with the idea of employing the written word to useful ends.

◆ Continue reading aloud to children even after they can read for themselves. They will still enjoy hearing stories that are at and above their reading level (and parents can always find something more advanced, yet still appropriate for children, to read aloud). Hearing books somewhat beyond their age level helps raise children's reading levels, without the frustration they'd encounter if they tried reading the same book on their own.

Parents also can perpetuate a climate of family closeness and safety this way—even bigger kids crave this. In the HomeArts network Internet article "Books Every Child Should Read: A Western Canon, Jr.," poet Rita Dove suggests that parents consider reading books at the same time as their children do when the children begin to think themselves too old to be "read to." This shared reading experience should be the jumping off point for parent-child discussions. Dove notes you may end up reading some books that wouldn't be your first choices, but again this represents an opportunity. Perhaps you and your child can take turns picking the books that will be shared. In this way, you can introduce some of the better-quality books you have in mind, or that you find on our list in the appendix.

◆ Unless there's a book you come across that you particularly want to read as a family—such as *The Lion, The Witch and The Wardrobe* by C.S. Lewis—try letting the child judge for himself what he wants to read on his own and what he wants you to read to him. Sometimes you'll end up doing both. Though some children push themselves to read difficult books, they'll usually speak up when they think a parent should read a more difficult book to them. But the beauty of a natural reading atmosphere is, *they'll seldom dismiss a book entirely.* Save 'til later, maybe—Allen will often say of a harder book we regard with raised eyebrows, "I'm going to try it." But even if it doesn't work out at the time, he won't dismiss it forever. The frustration factor that makes children think "no!" and "can't!" just won't be there.

◆ Setting specific times and places for reading aloud can be a good idea, because it gets to be habitual, and children respond well to the "certain times for certain things" mode. It also creates family rituals. When something is routine, children are more likely to quickly settle in and get in the mood.

However, too rigidly stressing that certain times are "reading times"—and thereby implying that others are not—would obviously be a mistake.

Sometimes, rigid reading times become like studying—too much like work. For reading to be habit, setting specific times can help. But for reading to be a lifestyle, to become second nature, the activity must more often be spontaneous. It's great when the family hits a quiet spell, and someone wonders aloud, "What can we do?" and the suggestion to read a book or start a new one comes up, quickly. Further, if reading time is scheduled too strictly, it can become more a chore than a pleasure on nights when it's inconvenient.

◆ It's also important, to encourage older children to read aloud to younger ones (that's not to say the younger ones can't demonstrate their budding reading prowess, as well). Children reading to one another brings them and the family together. Especially if the children normally go in different directions, it might be one of the few opportunities in their daily lives to share a common experience. The older child can introduce the younger to his favorite stories. This is a wonderful way to facilitate respect for reading, and for one another, as well to give children the chance to leave their own "literary legacies." This also encourages pride in reading ability for older children.

In our son Riley's young life, we've already seen several examples of older child-friends giving him copies of their own favorite books as gifts. We thought this was a marvelous exercise because the children gave much more than a gift: they passed on pieces of their own literary history. And their faces showed how proud they were to do it.

Aside from the bonding opportunities children reading to siblings and other young friends creates, studies have shown that cross-age reading has very positive effects on the reading and learning skills of all parties involved. In Storymates, a nine-week program piloted in a Southeastern U.S. elementary school, administrators found that, for example, sixth-graders who read to kindergarten-age children became more interested in reading and writing themselves and would even spend their free time scanning library shelves for more books to read to the younger siblings and neighborhood friends.

The Storymates program, while limited in duration, seemed to have a ripple effect. Not only did the children being read to benefit by learning to listen, but some parents of the children involved reported that those younger children in turn were attempting to read aloud to *their* younger siblings and acquaintances, trying to emulate the older brothers and sisters. From this example, you can clearly see how the reading habit is easily perpetuated in families.

◆ The Storymates program also successfully linked reading at school to reading at home. Encourage your children to discuss books they're reading at school; and conversely, to share books they're reading at home with teachers and classmates (such as during Show and Tell or reading discussions if they are held). Some classes have actually formed "book clubs," in which students pair up and choose, read, and report on books together. Many of the books chosen in these clubs end up coming from the home shelves. Children are proud to recommend their own books—and best of all, to have others read their recommendations. Allen and his friend John are shining examples of this.

We'll never forget the day Allen finally convinced John to read some of the beloved Roald Dahl books from his personal collection, and how proud he was when John liked them.

◆ Carry books with you wherever you go. Designate a large canvas bag as the "book bag." It doesn't take much forethought to keep it full and remember to take it along. But you never know when you and your child will hit a traffic jam, or wait longer than expected at a doctor's office, or have a few spare minutes before school starts. Children who live between two parents, or who are enrolled in afterschool programs and other activities, really do end up carrying their books with them everywhere in school bookbags and backpacks.

The point is, always having books handy takes advantage of unexpected downtime. And it can work magic on your nerves in a stressful situation. Bits of reading serve as peaceful balm that stays with you throughout a busy day. Also, it feels good to accomplish something in a situation where you'd normally just sit and feel powerless.

◆ Offer books and encourage reading, but don't become obsessed with teaching a young child to read. Let her set the pace. The exposure to books and language from reading aloud, and the provision of good books with pictures to examine on her own, is enough to start with. Remember that reading well-chosen books aloud is a disguised teaching tool as well, and that this act has been shown to significantly, yet gently, increase reading ability. Jim Trelease agrees that when children are read to, their imaginations are stimulated, and their attention spans are stretched. In the meantime, their reading comprehension improves and emotional development is nurtured.

At the heart of it all, you want to create a bookish environment where children can be comfortable and move around. And remember that reading, on *any* level, is good. The very acts of reading, and listening, in themselves are what's important. (See Choosing Books Is More than Reading a Label, p. 65.)

Plato said: "Avoid compulsion and let early education be a manner of amusement. Young children learn by games; compulsory education cannot remain in the soul." Books should fall first and above all under the category of "amusement," even when the entertainment will enrich and build critical skills. The goal isn't to read difficult books; it's merely to discover good books that nourish the spirit and the intellect. And this should be fun.

◆ Visit the library at least once a week. Obtain a library card in your child's name. There's nothing more you can do to instill such a feeling of ownership than to give access to and therefore allow children to take home anything they want within the confines of a whole building! Or, if you live in a big city, a whole chain of them!

Becoming comfortable in book-filled places is important. Children can choose stacks of books and read silently in the library. You can take bills to pay, or your laptop computer, while your child does his homework there. Make it a haven.

Encourage children to interact with the librarians whenever possible. Teach them to turn to these helpers when they're looking for something in particular, or want to find books on certain subjects, or have questions as to where certain books are shelved. This not only promotes independence but involves the child directly in choosing his own books. Again, pride comes with this. And the whole exercise instills some much-deserved respect for hardworking and oft-underpaid librarians and their knowledge.

◆ Enroll children in special library programs, like story hours, if the schedule works for you. Often, library story hours are held on weekday mornings, which is impossible for most dual-career parents. But if you're a stay-at-home or work-at-home parent, try to make time in your schedule for these.

Also, don't forget to sign up your children for library summer reading programs that encourage at-home reading. Often, the number of books required to win the certificate and small prizes at the end of the summer is not burdensome, and you can parlay the whole experience into yet another opportunity to instill pride in reading and strengthening your child's identity as a reader. In fact, when we signed up Allen for our local branch library's program, we signed up one-year-old Riley as well. (The rules stated he was old enough, since it was permissible for other people to read the books to children too young to read for themselves. Allen designated himself as Riley's official reader. Guess who benefitted most from the program?)

In Celebration of the Library Card

In these days of souped-up bookstores, fancy book packaging, and platinum credit cards, the modest library card can seem pretty mundane. But consider what this completely free piece of plastic or paper can acquire, as opposed to other cards, all of which come with a catch. Just by flashing your library card to a librarian, or even entering your card number in an online library access program, you can procure any book within that entire library's system (and even from others through special loan programs). And if it's not on the shelf, or someone else has it, just name your title—or subject, if you're doing research—and *those librarians will find that book for you!* They might even send you a nice little postcard, or call you up, to let you know when it comes in. And then, best of all, you get to take it home and read it at your leisure ... for free! In essence, your lowly-seeming personal library card makes you a member of the universal body of literature.

It sounds dizzyingly important when approached that way, doesn't it? And it can to your child, too, if you get to him before the notion of "money spent equals better stuff" sets in. Most libraries require that children reach a certain age, usually six, or that they be able to write their names, for a library card to be issued.

When this occasion comes, make a big deal of it. Choose a special "library book bag." Spend time in the library together, reacquainting the child with his new domain, then max out the new card with books of his choosing. Take the family out for ice cream afterwards. Go over the library lending rules together. Sit down to read a few of the chosen books that same day. Designate a special place where the library books will be kept (so you and the child can keep track of them and their due dates).

Your child will glow with pride to have gained entrée into such a privileged society.

◆ Join the Friends of the Library, and participate in other library volunteer activities, if you are able. This demonstrates to your child your dedication to library causes.

An inspired, interactive Massachusetts library program grew from a Junior Friends of the Library chapter. In her May 1997 *School Library Journal* article "Lords of the Library," Donna Beales describes how administrators came up with a novel way to capture the imaginations of the juvenile members, and help the library at the same time. Children vowed to become "Knights of the Ring," a quest patterned after the actual steps medieval knight-wannabes had to follow. The children then were charged with "defending their castle"—in this instance, the library. Their duties included helping with library activities and performing reading and research assignments. Afterward, in a public "knighting ceremony," they received decorative rings. The program has been such a smash that it has spread to many other New England libraries and schools.

Bookstores also offer story hours and other activities to promote children's books. Some sponsor regular children's book signings and "appearances" by popular book characters. Children are often awed to meet their favorite characters "in person"—because they easily form relationships with characters they love. This is the kind of children's book marketing that actually encourages children to get more mileage and enjoyment out of the good books.

As long as you think the products are good, attend book-related events as often as you can. Many bookstores distribute event calendars to publicize their special programs. Always check these out to see what's going on. When a child can actually see the author, and even have her book personally signed, it's a big deal. And, you're helping instill some healthy respect for children's authors, and attaching some additional meaning to the book. This is a great exercise—so long as children do not begin to equate the acquisition of books with dropping a lot of money.

Building on these suggestions, a parent need only take the concept several steps further to encourage the reading of the best books out there. Finding and acquiring these books is discussed in other chapters. You'll find suggested book lists at the back of this guide.

How to Wean a TV Junkie—Or Avoid the Habit Altogether

◆ Reduce the number of TV's in use in your home. For instance, you might keep one in the family room, and one in your own room as a back-up. Many children have their own TV's, but we question that practice. If children are "treated" to their own bedroom TV's, it seems to send a message that TV is more important and desirable than perhaps it should be. Besides, this often segregates your family *by TV show!*—which is pretty silly and counter-productive to family time when you think about it.

Moreover, people who cut down their TV time often are amazed at how much free time they end up having left over. It can turn out to be an amazing gift of time for harried families.

Carl Sandburg, the famous Swedish-American poet and biographer—and also a writer of well-loved children's books, including *Rootabaga Stories*—was an early critic of TV. He called it the "idiot box" (until he realized he could watch live baseball games on it, during which he suspended that harsh judgment). So the Sandburgs did own a TV, but it usually sat cold in the corner while the family sat around the dinner table at their North Carolina home, listening to Carl read aloud from the head of the table. The Sandburgs even kept a toaster at tableside so they didn't have to leave the reading and go all the way to the kitchen to toast more bread. A bit eccentric, perhaps. But it says a lot for their literature-oriented household that the Sandburgs raised book-loving daughters who became writers themselves.

◆ If you can bear to part with cable television service yourself, consider canceling it or switching to a reduced package that offers better reception for several basic channels, including public television. It'll simply slash TV time by reducing the dazzling number of channel choices. Some parents, however, enjoy having high-end cable channels for themselves and their children, such as Disney, Discovery, and Nickelodeon (we like the Nick Jr. preschool programming early in the day, with inventive shows like *Gullah Gullah Island* and *Blue's Clues*).

If you keep the premium channels, videotape desired shows and let children view them at your discretion, so the programs do not encroach on time better spent doing family activities. (Also, stay on the look-out for interesting shows and movies the children might not be aware of. We've introduced Allen to several favorites this way. And, personally, we'd rather repeatedly see the 1970s cartoon version of *The Phantom Tollbooth* we taped once from the Cartoon Network, than endless mind-numbing cartoons airing back-to-back on real time.) Of course, *every* show doesn't have to be educational, but those of us who watched *Gilligan's Island* for years know nobody really needs endless hours of televised entertainment.

Through videos, you can shift the TV viewing times to ones that suit you—like when you're trying to concentrate on something else like work, dinner, or company, but don't want your children watching "whatever's on." In this way you can refuse to allow the TV either to disrupt the family schedule you set or become "filler." And your children still get to watch their shows.

Also, during times many parents most need the diversion for their children, such as early morning or before dinnertime, good children's programming is available on PBS. No one knows when the children are around better than PBS.

◆ What works for some families is creating a TV calendar, where family members fill in the shows they want to watch during the week. *PBS Families* magazine suggests that, after each chosen show, you turn the TV off. This way, the rules are set from the get-go. When you click off the TV, you won't (justly) be accused of being a total kill-joy. The children were party to the decisions to watch the shows and to forego the ones afterward. If a conflict arises, talk it over. Then discuss together how the problem might be approached the next time. This involves the children, and makes them feel more a part of the process, and you less of a censor (although in our family, since the children are young, we're fairly dictatorial about when the TV is off and when it's on).

Taking a child off heavy doses of TV is like withdrawal. Children forget what it's like to live without it. They often can't figure out what to do with the "downtime." Weaning the TV junkie requires a slow but steady approach, taking it one day at a time. *PBS Families* suggests you start by mandating the TV is off say, one night each week. You can help get children started by suggesting substitutions, from reading to completing homework, to other types of imaginative play, to helping *you*. In the next week or two, cut out another chunk of TV, and so on. Eventually, you'll see a pair of bright eyes emerge from behind that veil of glaze!

For more suggestions on controlling TV in your home, and preventing common misunderstandings and conflicting values that arise from the free reign of TV, order a copy of a book called Remote Control Childhood? Combatting the Hazards of Media Culture *by D.E. Levin, through the National Association for the Education of Young Children. Call 1-800-424-2460. The book, which is promoted by PBS, costs eight dollars.*

Life is too short for reading inferior books.

—James Bryce

Good Taste Is Learned

When you consistently read the work of talented writers, you become a keen judge of what constitutes good writing. Surely you can spot the difference between immensely popular and readable, but ordinary, writing like Barbara Taylor Bradford and Sidney Sheldon, and the multi-layered, moving work of modern-classic writers like Kaye Gibbons and Pat Conroy. Apply the same discerning eye to children's books.

Adults often fail to remember that children's books should be as well-written and interesting as the best grown-up books. Good children's authors don't write down to children; they just write in language children can understand and enjoy. They seek to capture their imaginations and engage their minds. Read the first couple of chapters of most any book listed in this one, and prove to yourself how much you already know about good writing. See the excerpt of Natalie Babbitt's *Tuck Everlasting* included in this chapter for an example of how good children's book writing can be.

Look at a children's book: are you impressed with the writing and the way the story is told? If it's won prestigious prizes or is so beloved it's become a classic, the answer probably will be yes. If you read a great many such books, you will acquire an eye and a taste for the best children's literature. And you'll be able to

Excerpt from *Tuck Everlasting* by Natalie Babbitt

The sky was a ragged blaze of red and pink and orange, and its double trembled on the surface of the pond like color spilled from a paintbox. The sun was dropping fast now, a soft red sliding egg yolk, and already to the east there was a darkening to purple. Winnie, newly brave with her thoughts of being rescued, climbed boldly into the rowboat. The hard heels of her buttoned boots made a hollow banging sound against its wet boards, loud in the warm and breathless quiet. Across the pond a bullfrog spoke a deep note of warning. Tuck climbed in, too, pushing off, and, settling the oars into their locks, dipped them into the silty bottom in one strong pull. The rowboat slipped from the bank then, silently, and glided out, tall water grasses whispering away from its sides, releasing it.

Here and there the still surface of the water dimpled, and bright rings spread noiselessly and vanished. "Feeding time," said Tuck softly. And Winnie, looking down, saw hosts of tiny insects skittering and skating on the surface. "Best time of all for fishing," he said, "when they come up to feed."

He dragged on the oars. The rowboat slowed and began to drift gently toward the farthest end of the pond. It was so quiet that Winnie almost jumped when the bullfrog spoke again. And then, from the tall pines and birches that ringed the pond, a wood thrush caroled. The silver notes were pure and clear and lovely.

"Know what that is, all around us, Winnie?" said Tuck, his voice low.

spot it easily when checking out new books that don't have shiny stickers flagging them (noting awards that, you'll learn, don't recognize every worthy book, for many different reasons). You'll quickly see that much of the genre fiction being cranked out today fails most, if not all, of these tests.

It's commonly recognized among the purists in the children's book industry that children's books must not only be as good as adult books—they must be better. Why? Because children are perceptive and shrewd. You can't fool them. That's why, if they're offered the best children's literature available, they'll soon be able to spot the shabby products. If they've always just read the mediocre material, they'll have no basis from which to judge. So in the act of finding these better books for them, whether it's with your library card or your checkbook, you'll actually unleash

"Life. Moving, growing, changing, never the same two minutes together. This water, you look out at it every morning, and it *looks* the same, but it ain't. All night long it's been moving, coming in through the stream back there to the west, slipping out through the stream down east here, always quiet, always new, moving on. You can't hardly see the current, can you? And sometimes the wind makes it look like it's going the other way. But it's always there, the water's always moving on, and someday, after a long while, it comes to the ocean."

They drifted in silence for a time. The bullfrog spoke again, and from behind them, far back in some reedy, secret place, another bullfrog answered. In the fading light, the trees along the banks were slowly losing their dimensions, flattening into silhouettes clipped from black paper and pasted to the paling sky. The voice of a different frog, hoarser and not so deep, croaked from the nearest bank.

"Know what happens then?" said Tuck. "To the water? The sun sucks some of it up right out of the ocean and carries it back in clouds, and then it rains, and the rain falls into the stream, and the stream keeps moving on, taking it all back again. It's a wheel, Winnie. Everything's a wheel, turning and turning, never stopping. The frogs is part of it, and the bugs, and the fish, and the wood thrush, too. And people. But never the same ones. Always coming in new, always growing and changing, and always moving on. That's the way it's supposed to be. That's the way it *is*."

For more about Tuck Everlasting, *see book list entry on p. 98 in the appendix.*

the innate ability they already have to tell the good literature from the cheap stuff.

Like adults with their magazines and beach blanket books, children need to indulge in their own "escape reading." They can't read at the apex of their level all the time. Part of the organic reading process is reading a great many things in the course of a day. Yet a reading diet that consists only of series books fails to provide enough literary substance.

It's important to remember good books aren't hard to read. "Better" doesn't mean "harder." For a beautiful, moving example of how good books can transform a child's life, check out *Cushla and Her Books* by Dorothy Butler, the story of a severely handicapped and presumed learning disabled child who was brought out of a painfully narrow existence by wonderful books that gave her the tools to find her place in the real world. (See the Bibliography/Recommended Reading section in the appendix.)

Some Tips to Put Your Child on the Right Path

Here are some tips on how to get children on the right reading path, and promote the reading of better books:

◆ If your child's basic choices seem below par, it's your job to step in and make some substitutions. Consult the list in the back of this book to help you choose books that better match your child's interests. Perhaps you just need to consider the broad genre, or maybe it's more a consideration of subject matter. (See Luring the Noninterested Reader and the Junk Book Junkie, p. 39.)

Talk to your child's teachers; they often have reading lists of their own that could help you in your quest. And skilled librarians can be masters at suggesting reading material. If your child has a penchant for reading about junior high romance, or mysteries, or horror, a dedicated librarian usually can recommend high-quality substitutes for hastily written best-sellers. (A starter list we've compiled from such librarian suggestions, called "Fresh Alternatives," can be found in the Emergency Genre Junkie Kit on p. 42.)

◆ Don't shy away from books written long ago, or those set in other time periods—either backwards or forwards. (See Whither the Classic? p. 35.) Many children seem to be drawn only to "contemporary" situations such as those in popular series books. Yet many of these same children could be enchanted by life-inspired classics such as the Little House books or, for older readers, *The Call of the Wild*.

The reason many books on our suggested list, though written decades back, are included is that, through the passage of time, there is proof they endure. The action, daily activities, setting and even characters' names may not be of our time (though it's remarkable how many "older" books are surprisingly non-dated). But you'll notice the themes, values, problems, and human situations are indeed the same. And they will remain so. Likewise, their stories remain amazingly relevant and even riveting to the most modern of readers. In the case of fantasy, such fresh new

Whither the Classic?

What makes a classic? Those of us in touch with our cultural and spiritual heritages can easily answer that question. It's the universal nature of the story. For Jews, the Passover story remains lively today and never grows old. For Christians, the story of the Prodigal Son continues to speak volumes about love and forgiveness despite its being set back in the time of Jesus. African folk tales, Aesop's fables, Native American legends, the teachings of Buddha—they all express universal problems.

Good literature is the same. Why do young girls still savor Frances Hodgson Burnett's *A Little Princess?* Why do George MacDonald's delightful fairy stories, circa 1800, seem as fresh and delectable as ever? Why do folk tales hundreds of years old still capture the imaginations of children today? Robert McCloskey's *Make Way for Ducklings* enchants today's children despite the distinct 1940s flavor of its drawings. And despite the passage of one hundred years since *The Adventures of Tom Sawyer* was written, children still thrill to Mark Twain's classic tales of a mischievous boy.

Good literature and good music are timeless. We still listen to Mozart, and Shakespeare's plays are performed every day, in many languages. You can still buy copies of every major recording the Beatles made—nearly thirty years after their breakup. Classics stand the test of time.

A writer doesn't need to discuss malls, television, and the Internet to strike a chord in today's children. Those are just the accessories to the characters and stories. After all, do you remember the jovial, hardworking character of Pa Ingalls, and his evening fiddling sessions, or the fact that he farmed with a team of plow horses?

worlds have been created—as in *The Hobbit* or *The Phantom Tollbooth*—that time is utterly and completely irrelevant.

Do stay alert, however, to the new books coming out, and give your children the opportunities to meet characters who dress, speak, eat, and play just as they do. The character Amber Brown from the popular chapter book series is a good example. But you'll be surprised at how little modern-day trappings can matter when a child learns to love story and substance—and true universal and timeless values—over the little superficial siren songs some popular books rely on even to be picked up: that sneaky, manipulative "See—*I* know what you're doing and what you like …" but giving them precious little else.

◆ Reading a first chapter aloud is a good way to get a child interested in one of your choices. First, make sure the book is active and engaging—and if it is, the child might well choose to finish the book herself, unless you specifically want to read the whole book together. It's easy to find time to read just one chapter to get a child started. Your introductory asistance can help lower your child's guard. And regularly reading the captivating first chapters of good books will prove to her what a good book is. Soon she will be "hooked."

◆ After showing your child the way with the above tips, assemble a pool of suggested books and let him make the choices. (For more long-term suggestions, see Building Your Magic Bookshelf, p. 57.) Through all your effort, you will have gained your child's trust. At the same time, allowing choices makes reading seem less of an assignment, even though the potential selections were actually gathered by you.

As we've discussed before, a major pitfall occurs when children see books as "homework." Except for the required book list issued on the last day of school, reading is often automatically turned off for summer and any other school break. Older children put reading materials in their lockers with their textbooks at the end of the day—a tragedy. But literature and reading for the joy of it never have to go away, not at the end of the school day, not for the summer. Approach reading as fun. Show pride in your child's selections and make a pleasant fuss over the choice of good books. Let the child become a book advocate who can tell you what makes one book superior to another.

◆ As you're making book selections and trying to encourage higher quality reading in your child's life, try not to be overprotective. If it's a well-respected book, the content is probably fine. Besides, if a book depicts a character dealing with the death of a pet or a family member—such as *Bridge to Terabithia* by Katherine Paterson, which handles the death of a best friend very sensitively—the child is exposed to a new experience, whether it's one he is facing or not. (Add in the fact that there are always private fears and worries parents never learn about. Thus, you can never know what subject matter might press a button or ease a mind.) On the flip side, don't mistake your concern that he reads better books for censorship.

Remember, literature is a way to prepare for life's experiences. After all, fiction is about the human condition and how we as humans cope with life. While the themes in books can seem troubling, think about how books have helped you in your understanding of the world. Good books do more than present situations, they create thought processes. They challenge and even force children to leave their assumptions behind.

You'll Find Your Own Way

Once you get going—and don't worry about "missing" every now and then, because children are individuals, after all—you'll likely become quite familiar with material that suits your child's reading abilities and interests at each particular stage. You'll have only to scan the first chapter or so of a book that's new to you, and thumb through the rest for word usage and content, to make an educated guess as to whether it will go over well. Don't forget to exploit all the books by a tried-and-true favorite author. Our chapters Choosing Books Is More Than Reading a Label on p. 65 and Building Your Magic Bookshelf on p. 57 describe this challenge in greater detail.

Even when checking out books completely unfamiliar to you, some will leap out: here's one about a kid who just got braces on his teeth; here's a book about a math whiz; here's one by a favorite, prolific author like Louis Sachar. It's gratifying when you get to the point where you can spot a winner almost immediately. (It also indicates that you've gotten to know your child well.)

And on a day that I remember it came to me that "reading" was not "the Cat lay on the Mat," but a means to everything that would make me happy. So I read all that came within my reach.
—Rudyard Kipling, from Something of Myself: For My Friends Known and Unknown

Luring the Noninterested Reader (and the Junk Book Junkie)

It's easy to acknowledge the benefits a child can reap from reading, and you can study the market, invest in all the best books, and devote lots of energy to making your household a more literate environment. But what if you have a child who, though his learning and fundamental reading skills appear adequate, shows no real affinity for reading, who just seems noninterested in books?

In this instance, we're not talking about the more delicate situations of a so-called "reluctant reader," in which a child's refusal to read might be connected to serious problems such as a learning disability, attention deficit disorder, attitude or discipline problems, or a general mental block. These conditions require the assistance of a specialized teacher, psychologist, or other person trained to offer solutions and treatment. Books that specifically address the problem of reluctant readers, such as *Parents Who Love Reading, Kids Who Don't: How it Happens and What You Can Do About It* by Mary Leonhardt, can help parents find resources to overcome such obstacles (see appendix).

However, a scenario where parents can successfully provide

their own home-grown assistance involves the normal-achieving student who just can't seem to lock in on books that inspire her. As a result, she becomes what we call a "noninterested reader." Such children are capable of reading on acceptable, even high, levels but will seldom read anything they don't have to. In short, they've never met good books they really liked.

To face this challenge, parents need to redouble their efforts to prove that "good books" are really good. Instead of trying to woo the child with something, anything, launch a search for a book so good, on such a tantalizing and relevant subject, that he can't help but be interested. Does he love Alaska? As a family, try reading aloud *The Call of the Wild* by Jack London, or Jean Craighead George's intensively researched adventure/coming of age novel, *Julie of the Wolves*, which is set in Alaska (and which has two sequels the child might then want to read on his own). Or, if your child reads on a young adult level, find him a copy of naturalist John Muir's personal account, *Travels in Alaska*. Start with a subject that turns your child on so much, a book about it is irresistible.

It's always struck us as backwards that the approach to dealing with non-reading children has often been to toss the lowest-level junk at them—as if mediocre material could possibly enlighten minds already skeptical that there's anything good out there.

In his *Read-Aloud Handbook*, Jim Trelease tells of a boy who recoiled when his neighbors' father interrupted playtime to sit down with the children for a read-aloud session. The boy was invited to join them but adamantly declined. The father good-naturedly told the boy he was welcome to wait outside if he wished, until they were finished reading. The boy was persuaded to linger in another part of the room with them, thought he stubbornly maintained that reading time wasn't for him. But gradually he started tuning in anyway—and became so captivated by *My Side of the Mountain* that he drew nearer and nearer until he was finally in the circle with the readers, eagerly listening to every installment and "happening" by the house promptly at reading time every evening. Soon after, he was spotted at the bus stop with his own copy of the book.

Here are some other points to keep in mind when dealing with a noninterested reader:

◆ As illustrated in the above anecdote, the best way to pique a child's interest often is by reading carefully chosen books to the child "in company"—either reading aloud one on one or with other family members or friends. To jump-start this habit, you can turn to Trelease's books on the subject.

Noninterested readers need to experience firsthand how exciting and enjoyable books can be, and like the skeptic in the anecdote, develop a thirst for more. The chosen books must be absorbing; the characters likable, funny, and adventurous; the plot suspenseful; and the end gratifying. This may sound like a tall order, but trust us: many books fit this description (to start, see the short list on p. 43, as well as our comprehensive list in the back).

◆ Keep in mind the books you choose don't always have to be fiction. For many children, nonfiction books that speak directly to their interests, like how-to or biographical works, can work the same magic. Some juicy children's nonfiction titles are listed at the back of this book.

Not every child is, or is meant to be, a bookworm. But there are many different kinds of books out there, and you can be sure there is something for every child that can delight and challenge.

◆ Help the child stay engaged by reading aloud alternate chapters of a book, especially with fiction, which is a more communal medium. You can take the first chapter, then the child can read the second, and so on. This can make reading seem more of a game and less of a task. It also gives a sense of accomplishment, as the reading generally goes faster with a little adult assistance. And it's also fun to create these memories.

◆ "Age-level" reading guidelines can be a big stumbling block for some children (see Choosing Books is More Than Reading a Label, p. 65). Children whose reading abilities are coming along, but still might not be as strong as that of their peers, can grow intimidated, even humiliated, and give up. With the support of their parents and the attention of academic professionals in their lives, this can improve.

For your part, you can find books written on slightly lower

Emergency Genre Junkie Kit

For some parents, the challenge lies not in getting a child to read period, but in challenging a reader who, say, adores pulpy horror, mystery, or young romance novels. If this is your situation, do a favor for the child who enjoys a good thrill by putting her hands on some well-written books with similar subject matter. There are many great choices that lurk behind the cheapies with the lurid covers. This isn't a highbrow concept. It's simply giving the child a better book.

For a solid middle-grade reader, a parent might look for a copy of *The House With a Clock in Its Walls* by John Bellairs, or another of his numerous ghostly-with-a-touch-of-cozy-comfort novels. Just as good is *The Ghost Belonged to Me* by Richard Peck, a book that sprang off into sequels just as hilarious and witty as the first. (See appendix.)

Parents partial to classics should also remember that *A Christmas Carol* by Charles Dickens is one of the best ghost stories ever written. Along the same lines, readers seeking multicultural themes might enjoy *The Dark-Thirty: Southern Tales of the Supernatural* by Patricia C. McKissack. Meanwhile, children in the early elementary grades (and their parents, who should make this a read-aloud choice just so they can enjoy it themselves) love the clever *Bunnicula: A Rabbit Tale of Mystery* by Deborah and James Howe. Even kiddie horror king R.L. Stine has named the superior *Bunnicula* as a personal favorite.

Once the shift is made to better books, it's possible the child might be willing to open his eyes to the wider variety of books out there, and branch out on subject matter as well. But tread lightly: don't berate the cheap books or snatch them away, insisting you have something much better for him than that. Try to casually leave the book with the child and say, "I've heard this book is really popular with lots of kids your age." This, of course, will be true.

Also, our book list in the appendix features many books that have given way to series, and they are so noted. Many children love to get to know a set of characters and then follow them from adventure to adventure, book to book, like the Betsy-Tacy and All-of-a-Kind Family series. But you'll find these series and others noted here differ from the product-driven ones in that they usually began with one promising book that naturally overflowed into sequels. You can easily spot the difference in writing and concept. However, perhaps mentioning that a book is part of a series will help attract a child who already has shown an affinity for genre books.

Fresh Alternatives

For young readers who rarely deviate from the cheaper pre-teen (and young adult) genre fiction—and adults who want to give them more choices—here are some delicious alternatives librarians often recommend. Don't forget to look for similarly themed books by the same authors (and confer with your city, county, and school librarians).

Real life and romantic adventure for the Sweet Valley/Babysitters Club crowd:

The True Confessions of Charlotte Doyle, Avi
A Gathering of Days: A New England Girl's Journal, 1830-32, Joan Blos (Newbery winner)
Seven Days to a Brand-New Me, Ellen Conford
The Eternal Spring of Mr. Ito, Sheila Garrigue
Journey to America, Sonia Levitin
The Boys Start the War, Phyllis Reynolds Naylor
Sarah Bishop, Scott O'Dell
Jacob Have I Loved, Katherine Paterson (Newbery winner)
The Truth About Mary Rose, Marilyn Sachs
The Witch of Blackbird Pond, Elizabeth George Speare (Newbery winner)

(Be sure to look under the Growing-Up Themes and Everyday Kids sections of our master booklist for more suggestions. See appendix.)

Mysteries and thrillers for spooky story fans:

Something Upstairs: A Tale of Ghosts, Avi
The Ghost From Beneath the Sea, Bill Brittain
Herculeah Jones mysteries by Betsy Byars (including *Dead Letter* and *The Dark Stairs*)
McMummy, Betsy Byars
A Gift of Magic, Lois Duncan
Wait Till Helen Comes: A Ghost Story, Mary Downing Hahn
The Amazing Power of Ashur Fine, Donald J. Sobol
Ghost Abbey, Robert Westall
A Ghost in the House, Betty Ren Wright

(See many more spooky story suggestions in the Mystery/Scary section of our master booklist. See appendix.)

levels, but that still match your child's specific interests. In fact, this is the whole concept behind the rapidly growing "Hi-Lo" (high interest level, low reading level) book programs used to help older children and adults improve their reading skills, and even learn to read from scratch. Using desirable subjects as your guide, launch a hunt for enticing yet simply and clearly written books that might seem more palatable to your child.

I believe that books should play a prominent part in children's lives from babyhood; that access to books, through parents and other adults, greatly increases a child's chances of becoming a healthy and happy human being.

—*Dorothy Butler, from* Babies Need Books

Book-Lovers From Babyhood

If you think babies are too young to enjoy books, and that you might just as well wait until your children know a few words before introducing books to them, you're mistaken. You could be losing precious one-on-one experiences with your baby. But you might well wonder, how are they to understand the stories? Well, they can't. So what's the point in reading them aloud? And newborn babies don't focus well or even have the ability to distinguish colors in the early months. So what good are brightly illustrated books to them?

Experts have long reported that even infants who don't yet understand spoken or written language still should be considered an important part of the reading community, according to Cathleen S. Soundy in her Spring 1997 *Childhood Education* magazine article "Nurturing Literacy with Infants and Toddlers in Group Settings." Their eventual language and communication abilities can depend on this early exposure. It's the words children hear early and often that set the foundation of literacy and shape communication skills for the rest of their lives.

Also, any new parent knows that media and medical community reports are teeming with hot information about how babies' brains are wired and influenced by their surroundings, and how synapses (brain connections) made within the first months of life are strengthened in proportion to infants' exposure to new experiences (chiefly through baby-level introduction to the fundamental cultural blocks—literature, art, and music—in simple, natural forms).

Despite such noble incentives, however, some parents might understandably feel self-conscious reading aloud to an infant. At least one mother has likened this activity to "reading to a wall." Although babies may not understand language in the clinical sense, they love the lilting rhythm of words. It's music to them. Most of all, they love to hear the voices of family members and familiar friends reading just to them. It creates a close, cozy, reassuring environment of trust, personal attention, and care. It's as soothing as a lullaby (and for those of us who don't sing, a darn good substitute).

Children's author Maurice Sendak credits the physical closeness of sitting on his father's lap during reading with starting his lifelong love of literature. That physical connection can easily translate your affection for reading to your child.

Perhaps the best way to introduce the *concept* of a book to a baby is to give her a durable book—made of board, vinyl, or fabric—as an everyday object to get acquainted with. Like many playthings, bright, simple book covers make effective early focusing points when babies start needing visual stimulation.

For these "get acquainted" purposes, choose books with bold pictures of familiar objects, people, and animals, with little or no text (such as Tana Hoban's wide-ranging visual series, starting with *What Is That?, Black on White,* and *White on Black*). Read or "discuss" them aloud frequently, or just look at them together. Give these books to the baby as often as you would a toy, to handle on his own when he's in his swing, stationary exerciser, or even in the tub (that's what the vinyl books are for).

Keep the baby's books within easy reach—always a little stack in the play yard, in the toy baskets, in the crib. Many libraries keep bins of board books for checking out, so you can bolster your supply. You'll be surprised one day to turn around and find your baby studying a book and turning its pages on her own.

You'll delight to find her dragging one of her books from her toy basket to play with. (See Nurturing the Reading Habit, Naturally, p. 17.)

By about age six or seven months, many babies are fascinated by photos of other babies—sometimes, as in our case, before they even make the transition to more colorful drawings of common objects. By about eight months of age, our son Riley was "reading aloud" the photo-illustrated board book *I'm A Baby!* by Phoebe Dunn, studying and gurgling at the vivid pictures of real babies doing various baby things. He would pat the stiff pages and coo to the pictures in a soft "reading" drone.

Riley vigorously preferred this book to any other of the many we showed him. So instead of continuing to renew it from the library, where we'd first found it, we decided to order it for his own fledgling library (see Building Your Magic Bookshelf, p. 57). Of course, as an adult, he probably won't remember this little book like he will his favorite books as a first- or third-grader, but it'll always be his first favorite book. And we do know a young girl who loved *I'm A Baby!* so much as a toddler, she could still recite it by heart at age seven.

Also by about age six months, many babies begin to delight in colors and bold shapes. Early childhood reading expert Dorothy Butler, in her books *Babies Need Books* and the landmark *Cushla and Her Books*, cites the simple and appealing books of Dick Bruna, as well as early ABC books, as great baby-to-toddler selections. (See *Babies Need Books*—listed in the Bibliography/ Recommended Reading section at the back of this book—for good, thoroughly researched book references and lists for babies. This book is also a must-read for year-by-year book introduction techniques for parents of babies and preschoolers.)

Of further appeal to babies are books with textures they can feel with their own little hands, such as the classic *Pat the Bunny* by Dorothy Kunhardt. Older babies enjoy 3-D books and those with liftable flaps and other novelties that encourage interaction.

Couple your offering of chewable "toy" books with frequent reading aloud from the "real" ones with paper pages. Because of their more fragile nature, these are read with parental supervision only until the child is old enough to be more careful with them. Many experts agree nursery rhymes are the best place to start. From birth, babies enjoy patterned language, the cadence and rhyme and repetition in these verses. With your voice performing this symphony, it's bliss for a baby. Therefore, perhaps the best place to begin a new baby's library is with a big, colorful book of nursery rhymes that your child will grow into. (You'll find some suggestions on the master book list at the back of this book, and more in *Babies Need Books,* and *The Read-Aloud Handbook* by Jim Trelease.)

Experts recommend getting started by reading verses and poetry to babies for a few minutes each day. This is a pleasant, one-on-one way to share time and get acquainted with a new baby—you can do it while nursing, rocking, anywhere. Since the baby won't understand the material, you can branch out and choose works that sound nice and encourage interesting voice inflections, but are fun for *you,* whether it be classic children's poems by A. A. Milne or *The Rubáiyát of Omar Khayyám.* If you enjoy the activity, you're far more likely to indulge in it more often (not to mention the fact that babies are mirrors of your emotions; they can sense when you're bored or uncomfortable).

Similarly, oblivious as they might seem, babies pick up on such acts of love and nurturing. Before long, you might start to notice the baby reaching out for the book and patting it, even seeming to recognize and really look at familiar pictures. He might smile when he hears familiar rhymes—which, by the way, are great for reciting any time, from diaper-changing to walks in the stroller to driving in the car. Memorize a battery of rhymes if you haven't already.

A word of caution: if you wait for an infant to show a marked interest or reaction to books or poetry you read aloud to her, you'll likely be disappointed. Don't wait for reactions, nor give up. Offer babies frequent readings at odd moments, in small doses. Eventually, you will be rewarded with smiles in response to the soothing sound of your voice speaking familiar lines in lilting language, just for her.

As for older babies, parents know that even toddlers playing on the floor, seemingly absorbed in their play, are soaking in more than meets the eye. And when small children are used to reading aloud as part of their environment, you can bet they learn to enjoy and participate in it. After months of rudimentary reading exercises, we were stunned and delighted when, shortly after he turned one year old, Riley began pulling his standard favorites out of his board book piles and handing them to us to read to him. We thought, "He's got it!"

All this effort isn't just for the baby. You can enjoy these read-aloud sessions just as much, through sharing favorite rhymes and prose with your baby, looking at sharp-contrast pictures together, and getting acquainted with new children's books you've never seen. Some adults who find themselves not knowing quite what to say to a new baby find books a welcome medium, a concrete avenue through which to relate to a child instead of feeling compelled to spew out meaningless baby talk.

Perhaps best of all, parents and guardians who are rediscovering cherished favorite books and delighting in finding new books realize that having children gives them a second chance to sail into the magical world of juvenile literature.

We must try as best we are able to give our children words that will shape their minds so they can make those miraculous leaps of imagination that no sinless computer will ever be able to rival—those connections in science, in art, in the living of this life that will reveal the little truths. For it is these little truths that point to the awesome, unknowable unity, the Truth, which holds us together and makes us members one of another.

—Katherine Paterson, from Gates of Excellence: On Reading and Writing Books for Children

The Bond Between Reading and Writing

Reading and writing. They are the apple pie and ice cream of education. And yet, as grown-ups, we easily forget the strong connection between these two skills. One naturally leads to the other. Marie Clay, a past president of the International Reading Association, made a strong argument for the linking of these skills by noting that the single greatest predictor of reading success in the third grade is a child's breadth of experience with writing by kindergarten age.

Reading gives us something to say when we write. For children first wading into the realm of writing, reading will be the basis for the stories they craft. Adults will see that, in seeking inspiration for their own writings, children often begin by "borrowing" characters, plots, situations, literary devices, and language from their favorite books. Sharp creative writing skills are far easier to achieve when your imagination is already burning with illustrations of good writing from the books you've read. These books will always serve as shining examples that can illuminate a lifetime of written communication.

Looking at it this way, we can realize why we must take our efforts to advocate good books so seriously. Fine writing pro-

Internet Resources for Young Writers

Many resources for young writers and readers can be found on the Internet. After all, the means to communicate on the Internet is writing and reading. The Web offers a great basic language lesson: the more clearly you write, the more clearly your message will be received and understood.

Here is just a sampling of the treasure trove of writing- and reading-oriented Internet sites your child can journey to. (Please bear in mind that though these addresses were current at this book's press time, website addresses often change quickly and without notice. Please let us know if you have difficulty reaching a site, and we'll try to help.)

Young Writers' Clubhouse—An engaging site for children to learn about publishing opportunities and contests, join critique groups, and generally join the community of young writers.
http: //www.realkids.com/club.shtml

KidPub—A self-publishing center for children to publish and read other children's stories online.
http://en-garde.com/kidpub/intro.html

Inkspot for Young Writers—An offshoot of the adult Inkspot, where children can work on the craft of writing through tips and feature stories, engage in discussions with other young writers, and learn about places to publish original work.
http: //www.inkspot.com/joe/young/

WritingDEN—A site for sixth graders and older students to work on their writing and language skills.
http://www2.actden.com/writ_den/

vides concrete examples children can admire and even subconsciously emulate. But reading good books helps writing on a basic mechanical level as well. Children who read easily master usage rules, such as setting quotation marks and semicolons. Cheap fad books, with an emphasis on overly simple sentences and concepts, cannot create this familiarity with the mechanics of excellent writing.

In the March 1997 issue of *The Reading Teacher*, Peter J. Lancia demonstrates how children use stories they like as models for their own work. Children will draw on characters from favorite books and sometimes even actual stories they have read when they are assigned to write stories themselves. Lancia points out that few children do their literary borrowing by actually retelling a story they've read or heard. Some do, but most push to add their own embellishments and ideas. These mild "artistic thefts" actually create successful writing projects for budding authors, Lancia says. Indeed, these efforts soon develop into creative stories that rely less on the works of others.

Janie remembers trying to copy the writing style of Louisa May Alcott, even going so far as to sign her school papers "Jo" (after the lead character in *Little Women*—who is, interestingly, a book character so many girls of all types and ages seem to identify with. Perhaps it has to do with the fact that Jo is a writer).

Newbery-winning author Katherine Paterson has said that, as a college student, she would noticeably imitate the style of whomever was the subject of a particular paper. Of course, these early attempts later gave way to the individual style and strikingly original stories that have brought Paterson such acclaim. But her high standards were set in place long before she embarked on her first novel.

Testimony such as this and research like Lancia's provide all the more reason for parents to actively help their children choose good books. At best, poor quality literature that is plain and unimaginative will make your child's first writings seem flat and lifeless. Her ideas will lack spark and her stories will probably leave her unsatisfied with what she writes. The best writing stems from rich literary experiences. Books that are well written with descriptive language give your child a rich palette of ideas and examples to dabble in when it comes time to put words on a page.

Writing begins with ideas. Think about the great speeches you've heard in your life. Didn't it seem as if the writers of those speeches were extremely well read? A recent collection of speeches and daybook entries from Robert Kennedy, edited by his son Maxwell Taylor Kennedy, reveals the rich literary nature of Robert Kennedy. In *Make Gentle the Life of This World: The Vision of Robert F. Kennedy*, we see how the well-thumbed pages of Greek classics, Albert Camus books, and other literary works directly translated into the inspiring words of a popular politician. Kennedy, like many other lawyers, turned to Shakespeare and other classics when he needed to bolster a forceful argument. And how many sermons have you heard that featured literary references as a central theme? Clever writing begins with reading good material.

Just as sad as a childhood devoid of enjoyable literary treasures is the scenario of a child with no ideas of his own because he has read nothing of imaginative or creative value. Writing will be nothing but a joyless chore for the student who has no ideas to fuel his mind. Those blank pages will seem intimidating, and your child will soon believe he simply has no talent for writing.

Many experts advise parents to make good reading and productive writing parallel from an early age, and thereby indelibly imprint this link. Allen used to "dictate" letters to his grandparents long before he could write them for himself. Richard would type the letters into the computer verbatim and decorate them according to Allen's specifications with pictures of dinosaurs and airplanes. But Allen was driving the actual communication. These early "writing" efforts made what he had to say special—and permanent—when officially typed on a page. Later, when he became a reader, Allen easily shifted to typing his own letters.

Janie's grandfather gave her a manual typewriter to use when she was a young girl, in about the second grade. This device created many a Chapter One for her early efforts at writing. This awareness of "Chapter Ones" was, of course, inspired by Janie's own reading of chapter books. In her home, reading and writing were always encouraged as meaningful activities.

Parents and guardians can do more than they might think to encourage the reading-writing link. Even before he can write, your child can tell stories. When you read a good book, ask your child if he can tell you a similar story about something that happened to him. A good place to start for inspiration might be with the Mercer Mayer classic *Just Grandma and Me*. This charming book describes a boy's delightful day at the beach with an adorable grandmother. Maybe your child could tell you a story about his own favorite day with a grandparent or another special person. Make it even more special by having him dictate the story to you. Write or type the finished version neatly and perhaps even make it into a "book" complete with pasted-in pictures of the grandparent or other special person.

In *Raising Lifelong Learners*, Lucy Calkins notes that her children keep a notebook open to a blank page while reading books. When something strikes a memory of their own experiences, they jot down all their thoughts about it, and soon entire notebooks are filled. Calkins urges you to have children write something every day in a notebook.

Having children keep personal journals, and perhaps even posting books they've read to the journals, can also be inspiring ways to spur the creative process. You can use good writing in a specific book to show your child how it's done. If your middle-grade child struggles to add details to his writing, choose a descriptive passage from a favorite book to show how skilled writers use details to communicate more powerfully. (For a good example, see the excerpt from Natalie Babbitt's *Tuck Everlasting* on pp. 32–33.)

Tie together reading and writing at every turn. Even the most mundane activities can become simple and fun exercises. Let your child make out the grocery list (many children are eager to "help" like this anyway), or post upcoming events to the family calendar. Buy colorful note paper pads for every telephone station in your home, and help get children in the habit of writing down phone messages instead of shouting them down the hall to you— or worse, forgetting them.

Of course, all of this requires you as a parent to see that fine line between what seems like constant homework, and the true joy, empowerment, and convenience of reading and writing. This is especially true if you're trying to introduce a reading and writing lifestyle in your household when your child is older than, say, preschool age. But these early efforts to bind reading and writing will make your child an effective communicator throughout her life. Writing and reading will blend into well-developed critical thinking skills as she grows older.

With a Magic Bookshelf full of excellent writing examples, your child will always have inspiration close at hand. He also will recognize good writing and strive to write well in projects from journals to creative stories to routine exercises, whether at school or home.

A good book respects a child's intelligence, his pride, his dignity, and most of all his individuality and his capacity to become ...
—Jean Karl, From Childhood to Childhood: Children's Books and Their Creators

Building Your Magic Bookshelf

A Magic Bookshelf, other than the one imprinted on a child's memory, is the permanent shelf of tangible books she loves and can touch, books that reassure and delight her, books that challenge her imagination and intellect and will help shape her mind until she's ready to leave childhood and embark on the journey of her adult life. A Magic Bookshelf is crammed with books that, one after the other or at different periods of childhood, strike home with the child. At the very least, they become proud possessions.

So while much of your Magic Bookshelf may very well be with you always in your mind's eye, remember that a real bookshelf in your child's room is a must. The power of ownership is tremendous. It doesn't matter if it's just a handful of books; the pride your child will take in books that are "mine!" is visible in his eyes. Have a bookshelf or special place set aside in your child's room that allows him to display these proud possessions. Make a fuss over his books and say, "Let's read one of *your* books at bedtime."

All of this makes the bookshelf in your child's room or the family room much more important than those in the public library or bookstores. The home shelf contains the child's permanent book collection, the one she reaches into to while away idle moments, to retreat to in a time of solitude, or to close the day. And it should be viewed as a collection, because that is what it is—not just a jumble of books that were acquired and thrown together. Calling it a collection adds to her pride in reading.

Moreover, a child trusts and respects someone who makes an effort to find books she likes, and who has the ability to recommend a book she ends up adoring. Fill up a shelf with books like these and you'll have a lifelong and grateful reader.

Also, certain books on a Magic Bookshelf might bear sentimental meaning because they were given a child by a special person—a parent, friend, or relative—or which serve as "literary legacies" left by parents and other special people. (See Leaving Your Own Literary Legacy, p. 12.)

Other sections of this book can help you discern what books your child might embrace, according to personal taste and past successes, but you'll acquire books in many other ways. You'll want to bolster your child's physical library by gradually acquiring meaningful, well-written books he can enjoy continuously, visit often in childhood, and appreciate having when he grows older. If you enjoyed books as a child, you can look back now and see how you viewed them as old, faithful friends, clichéd as it seems.

The foundation for your child's bookshelf can be placed early on, and it's often free! You probably received many books as gifts throughout your childhood, and more probably will be given to your own child over the years. Adult gift-givers often instinctively choose books as a sentimental, important present, especially if they know they are contributing to a permanent collection. The well-chosen ones can be the finest assets of a child's book collection. Often lovingly inscribed with messages such as "Christmas 1999," or some other meaningful date, these books represent gifts from the heart, besides serving as mementos of special days in your child's life. Best of all, many gift books are classics.

Other additions to the shelf will be the books your child brings home from school book programs like Reading Is FUNdamental and high-quality children's book clubs you might subscribe to on your own. A mail-order book club can offer a solid core of good looking hardcover or softcover books that form the hub of a collection. The most fun and sense of accomplishment lies in constructing and continually building on the Magic Bookshelf yourself; but book clubs are a great place to start and offer regular surprises that are fun for parents *and* children. (See the appendix for book club and catalog suggestions.) Also, Troll Books and Weekly Reader book ordering programs are available in most schools. Many schools and churches sponsor one or two book fairs a year.

Add to these library book sales, used book stores, retail book stores with large children's book collections (some with fabulous discount sections, where you can walk away almost every time with a three- or four-dollar treasure), and yard sales.

In addition, many grocery stores stock children's books, especially new paperback editions of classics, or works with religious themes. These are often inexpensive and located in the point of purchase area next to the candy bars. In fact, buying books can actually leave you and your children satisfied during the often stressful moments that arise at checkout time. Perhaps, instead of a cheap plastic toy, you can let your child choose an inexpensive book—less than five dollars—once a month or so.

Yet here's the perennial question: you know where the books are, but how do you choose?

How to Choose Books for a Magic Bookshelf

You can start by re-reading your old favorites, then checking out some of the newer children's books that have received some attention. Caldecott and Newbery award winners can be a good place *to start*, mainly because they're easy to find, often set off in their own sections in stores and libraries. Award book lists are at the back of this guide. But, with these prize books must come a word of caution that for every winner, there are hundreds of other award-worthy books that do not have the benefit of such recognition. And it always stands that although a book may be considered "excellent" by adults, children have their own tastes. They like some and eschew others.

The master list in the back of this book includes suggestions

---

Books Are Investments

Your book purchases are investments, and the dividends are intelligence and imagination. A trip to an amusement park is a one-shot deal; so is an evening at a pizza parlor, in which you don't walk away with much other than a full stomach and perhaps some plastic trinkets. With books, you can spend the same amount of money—often less—and enjoy the treat over and over, forever.

---

for a body of books to start with. Many are considered as good or better than the award winners. Choose some to read, scan, or flip through on your own. Such background reading can provoke nostalgia, and reignite your own excitement in children's literature while you search for books your children might enjoy. There will always be "misses," but you'll be surprised at how well your instincts work to select good books for your child. After all, you know your child and her tastes better than anyone, including the award panels. And you know good writing. Just because a book is written for a younger person doesn't mean your taste can't discern what is well written for children.

Whether at retail stores or second-hand shops, try to acquire books that you think your child will truly *enjoy*. Look for fun, inspired, and imaginative stories. The best books, such as those represented in our book list, have a common quality: they have great stories that are fun to read. The most gorgeous volume of morality tales might not hold a candle to a well-worn John Bellairs paperback in a child's mind.

The most economical way to conduct personal taste litmus tests is to go to the library first. Check out books, or sit on a library sofa together, and notice which ones your child latches onto. As Jim Trelease suggests, after checking out a book for the umpteenth time, you should consider purchasing it. This is one of the most organic, and meaningful, ways to form the core of a child's Magic Bookshelf.

As a further aid to your search, many periodicals and a few TV shows review books for children. From the PBS show *Reading Rainbow*, you can get ideas for books your child might like—and if your child watches with you, you get a direct reaction before leaping into a purchase. Publications that review children's literature are listed in the further reading section at the back of this book.

Occasionally you might need to locate a special-topic book, such as one that addresses a developmental or psychological issue like dealing with a death in the family, divorce, adoption, new siblings, dyslexia, and so on. A prime resource available in many libraries is *The Bookfinder*, a two-volume tome that lists thousands of children's titles, cataloged by subject.

When building your shelf, don't neglect to add books of short stories. Early readers love these books because they come in big-kid looking thick volumes, but developing readers can still start and finish a whole story in one sitting, like *Sideways Stories from Wayside School* by Louis Sachar. Start with a collection like *Winnie-the-Pooh* by A.A. Milne, because they appeal to very small children and make for cozy read-aloud material. (Check the master book list for other short story suggestions.)

By the time she reaches high school, your child might well have hundreds of books.

How to Find Good Books in a Bookstore

Good books have common elements, regardless of genre or reading level. In theirMarch/April 1997 *Horn Book Magazine* article "Have Book Bag, Will Travel: A Practical Guide to Reading Aloud," Mary M. Burns and Ann A. Flowers outlined these attributes as including clearly defined themes; logical, suspenseful plots with few or no flashbacks (although we think books like *The Children of Green Knowe* by L.M. Boston are exceptions, because they handle timeshifts so skillfully and compellingly); memorable characters; and a problem that needs solving. Add to this plenty of action and intrigue to keep readers interested.

Such books are child-centered, but never cutesy. The well-told stories offer security, and often empower the child without preaching down to him. Your understanding of the basic elements of good stories will help you, then your children, make sense of the books they read. That's why it's so important to find books with the characteristics we just listed.

However, there's a big difference between looking for books

in a library and finding them in a store. You can fill a bag with library books at no risk. If your child doesn't like a book, you can just take it back. But long-term value is assigned to a store-bought book, especially when you're trying to stock a Magic Bookshelf on a budget. Here are a few tips:

◆ Choose stores with well-developed children's book sections that the booksellers obviously have invested effort in. Mall book shops and other bestseller-oriented chains, while convenient, usually don't have the enticing children's book sections you need. Also, don't forget that independent booksellers often feature excellent, lovingly chosen book sections. Identify these special stores and carve out large chunks of time for your expeditions to them. You need the leisure to browse; finding desirable books requires thought.

When you hear of a book you want to acquire but can't find, consider ordering it from an Internet bookseller like Amazon.com, which offers a trove of hard-to-find, rare, and backlist books along with the big sellers. Its capacity for "stocking" books seems unlimited. As opposed to a bookstore ordering the book for you and sometimes taking weeks, Amazon.com often will ship your book first class in a couple of days.

◆ Planning unhurried book-shopping trips also gives children the leisure time to peruse the shelves on their own. In this way you can gauge a child's interest before buying a book. Bookseller Terri Schmitz, in herMarch/April 1997 *Horn Book Magazine* article "'Tell the Lady What You Like': Shopping for Children's Books," suggests trying out your choices on younger children before you purchase. Also, you can verify you like them too—because if they go on your Magic Bookshelf, they'll be around forever. And, if your child is very young, you'll read them many times.

However, be mindful not to subconsciously cater to your own tastes instead of your child's. Many people, ourselves included, sometimes buy a particular book thinking a child will love it, because we did or think we would have. Sometimes it works. But it might not always be a certain child's choice. Some books will just miss. It's not a big deal—just move on. Don't fault your judgment too much, unless you seem to miss more often than hit. If that happens, you might, in fact, be catering to your own taste's instead of your child's.

◆ Many large bookstores are set up for reading, and are furnished with comfortable chairs and carpeted areas for stretching out. Small, independent stores will often have reading areas too. Visiting a cramped book area with a small child is not fun or practical for obvious reasons, nor is it productive. Choose stores that make you want you to relax and stay a while, and where sales clerks don't glare when you thumb through a book and then put it back on the shelf. You're not going for impulse buys anyway. The only time you'll shop in a hurry is when you're looking for specific titles.

◆ When enlisting the help of a book salesperson, give her some details. A question such as "What do you recommend for children?" is likely going to be answered with a pair of raised eyebrows, a sigh, and a patient answer that children are not all alike in taste, age, reading level, or in any other way. Terri Schmitz further points out that there is no battery of books that will suit every child. This is true of classics, too, of course. (That's why our master book list suggests a mix of current books and older favorites.)

Describe to the salesperson your child's personality, interests, and age, and if possible, name authors and books the child already enjoys.

◆ Try not to become too bogged down with the issue of reading level. (See Choosing Books Is More Than Reading a Label, p. 65.) You might encounter some salespeople—and occasional librarians too—who insist certain books are below, or above, the reading level for children of your child's age. Bear in mind that however well-meaning—there are many professional people who heavily subscribe to the "reading level" system—the salesperson doesn't know your child like you do. He doesn't really know the books your child will like to read, and he doesn't know what books you would like your child to read.

Also, remember salespeople are there to sell. Therefore, you can't blame them for trying to make a sale (although they should at least try to help you find what you want first). Many people who work in children's sections—unless they were stuck there to cover for someone else—regard children's books as special, too.

Just keep all your book-choosing criteria in mind while you shop. A more expensive book like the novelty book with the whirligigs, opening doors, and flashing lights, isn't necessarily better than a simple softcover with a wonderful story. After all, it's the story that truly fires the imagination.

Each reader is a judge. And he must look for that which serves him. He must find those books that lift his spirits, enlighten his mind, entertain his dull hours pleasurably, and lead him into new ventures of the imagination.
—*Jean Karl,* From Childhood to Childhood: Children's Books and
Their Creators

Choosing Books Is More Than Reading A Label

We live in an age in which decisions are made for us. We want it to be so. Go to your local toy store and walk down the aisles, and notice how all the boxes are labeled with specific ages for which the toys are appropriate. When did parents lose the ability to decide what toys are "right" for their children? Surely you've noticed your children showing no interest at all in "age-appropriate" toys, while playing with toys for children either much older or much younger.

Likewise, the most popular way of categorizing books these days is by age-level. Publisher's catalogs, book reviews and book lists, and sometimes even the covers of the books themselves, state: "Ages six-eight" or "Grades four-six," much like the packaging of toys.

But what about the eight-year-olds who read on what might be labeled an "Ages ten-twelve" level? Or the eleven-year-olds who struggle a little more, but are attracted to books on the "Ages eight-ten" level? Are all children of the same age, the same? Of course not. That's why this system can inadvertently work against them. Slower-reading children might become demoralized or ashamed by being designated as "behind," or, further, be deterred from reading books "below their level" that could be terrific reads. All because they (and perhaps their parents) think they're intended for younger children. Meanwhile, an advanced nine-year-old reader stuck in the "fourth-grade level" zone might not know how to put her hands on books that might be more meaningful to her.

Here's the deal: there are great books out there for *everybody*. It doesn't matter if your child is eight and loves a book a five-year-old might like also, or if a ten-year-old wants to try out *The Hobbit*.

Don't give up your parental authority and instinct when it comes to books. Your instincts, along with those of your children, are probably the best indicators of the right reading level for your child. The labels on books are often no more helpful than those on toy boxes. Blindly following those recommendations, other than using them as a general ballpark measure, could rob your child of some wonderful reading experiences either above or below his so-called "reading level."

Thus, the most important question is not, "How old is my child?" but, "What is my child's ability?" Follow that question by asking what books would best allow you to stretch that ability and enrich the thinking process. A quick scan of the first chapter or two of potential book choices gives the best indicator of what level the book is written for—not the age guideline on the bookstore shelf.

Here's something else to keep in mind: gauge *interest level* above all, even over skill. Ultimately, it doesn't matter whether a child can read something well if she doesn't relate to the book. Strong interest in and enjoyment of the material are the only ways to truly cultivate a dedicated reader. A boy who loves cars will quite likely be interested in a well-researched book about cars that happens to be a "level" or two below that prescribed for his age. In this case, it's the subject matter he seeks. What a shame for him to be too embarrassed, or reluctant, to pick it up, because of all those artificially imposed levels. Or, even worse, never to see it in the first place.

The book lists at the back of this guide are cataloged in general terms of baby and toddler books, picture books, early readers, chapter books, middle-grade novels, and advanced novels, along with nonfiction, short stories, and poetry. Where warranted, certain reading ability guidelines are added, and, we hope, enough description so you can glean whether or not the book might interest your child. However, for all the reasons above, there are no specific age- or grade-level designations.

Moreover, you may remember what a great pleasure it was in your childhood years to occasionally revisit a level of reading you'd mastered thoroughly. This is sort of a literary "comfort food." That is probably why many children like to read to younger siblings or other children, or "teach school." It allows the readers—or the teachers, as it were—to retreat to familiar territory and bask in the sense of confidence this brings. At the same time, it gives children the opportunity to leave their own literary legacies. (See Leaving Your Own Literary Legacy, p. 12.)

Children who are encouraged to reach into the whole pool of literature, and aren't pushed too hard to stay within the slim confines of a one-level-fits-all system, will likely be undaunted by the prospect of trying to read above their present abilities. The worst that can happen is they'll find themselves a bit over their heads and, without panic, paddle back to shallower waters. Unless these voyages give way to constant frustration, we think this is healthy. But bear in mind literature doesn't have to be over anyone's head to flex thinking patterns. The simplest books can present challenging ideas. Your ultimate goal is to expand your child's mind.

A good story is a good story regardless of the age level assigned to it. Your task at first should be to get your child to read material that inspires thought, which requires you to judge your child's progress and readiness for particular books. The goal isn't to measure your child's vocabulary and skills on some imaginary scale.

Without a doubt, this represents a lot of work. Being a parent is often hard, thankless work. But if you choose a book your child truly enjoys, then you will have that all-important "thank you" when you hear her enthusiastic review. Every giggle over a funny part and every tear shed at a sad part—and every "Just one more chapter, okay?" at lights-out—will quickly repay the effort.

Remember how hard your child is working, too. Learning to think and reason is hard. During these years, your child will build all the foundations for how he will later view the world. Remember this, and your part will seem much more meaningful. With reading and learning, you touch the future and make your child a better person. This is much too important to leave to other people. That's why picking what is "appropriate" for your child at a certain age should be your job. Sure, let the experts help with broad age- and grade-level advice. But reserve the final decisions for you and your child. After all, who do you want to influence the path your child takes? Strangers? Or, would you rather it be your involvement that sets the course your child takes toward advanced literacy?

Children are meant to grow up, and not to become Peter Pans. Not to lose innocence and wonder, but to proceed on their appointed journey ... Their books, like their clothes, should allow for growth and their books at any rate should encourage it.
—J.R.R. Tolkien, from Tree and Leaf

How To Choose A Book— A Child's Way

Ask a child what she looks for in a book, and the answer will usually be vague (it is, after all, a subjective decision). But in a child's view, usually the most important first characteristic of a "good" book is, not surprisingly, the cover.

Children are attracted to flashy, colorful objects. Books are no exception. Parents of children who read picture books have this a bit easier—most picture books are as, or more, remarkable for their art as for their prose. Thus, attractive art can lure a child to a well-conceived, well-written picture book. Older readers, however, often only have the completely separate cover art to attract them. Your challenge is to move them beyond that.

Following are some ideas to remember when you look at books for older readers, from the child's perspective.

◆ The main draw for those popular horror series books is that awful, exciting cover art, with garish colors and shiny foil lettering, and sometimes even a creepy 3-D hologram. Talk about powerful magnets for children! No wonder the series-du-jour books jump off the shelves. In fact, the most recent edition of the classic book, *Bunnicula: A Rabbit Tale of Mystery,* even has a jacket that looks very much like a Goosebumps book. A bunny's being suspected of being a vegetable-juice-sucking vampire is not as scary a concept as, say, a knife-wielding ghost. But the title is raised in foil, and the cover indeed makes the book appear scarier than it is.

However, if this makes children attracted to reading *Bunnicula*, more power to the plenty-powerful publishers. Perhaps publishers are learning how to make their old standards better able to compete with the fad books. And that's a good thing.

Janie can remember frequently checking out a middle-grade library novel by Constance C. Greene called *Isabelle the Itch*, which had a great cover, with a colorful picture printed directly on the smooth hard surface, a shady street scene, she recalls. The book could well have been a great read, but Janie doesn't know because she never bothered to read past the first few pages. That book facade itself was just such a winner, it felt good to possess it for a couple of weeks.

◆ New editions of the older classics—paperbacks with modern cover illustrations depicting, say, a hipper Alice in Wonderland with an updated outfit and trendier hair, compared with Sir John Tenniel's solemn Victorian Alice—can be a way to attract a child. The book is the same, but the cover is "better," or simply more modern. Similarly, that beautifully bound hardcover collector's edition of *Little Women* is wonderful to have on the shelf, but a softcover version with the four March sisters in colorful gowns, gaily singing 'round the piano (never mind that the book reveals the girls' gowns are faded and much-mended, and the piano out of tune) is probably more likely to be tossed in a backpack. Keep this trick in mind as you shop, and let the fancy volumes serve as "gift books." (See Building Your Magic Bookshelf, p. 57.)

◆ When you finally convince your child that he can't judge a book by its cover—which most children, in growing to maturity, will have to reluctantly agree is true if they learn to tell good writing from bad—he's probably going to move on to the next superficial aspect of a book: the inside flap or the back cover. But book blurbs are written and designed by: guess who! Those clever book merchandisers. Adult book blurbs with their fluffy, overblown praise, have become a joke, and adults perusing books usually know almost any book publisher can find at least one obscure review bit for a book—never mind who penned it—that includes the ecstatic proclamation, "An amazing work!" or "One of the ten best books of the year!"

Children's book blurbs are not much different, although there may be a hint more sincerity. But they are, after all, intended to enhance sales. Children at the very least get an idea of the subject and plot from the blurb. Just remember to teach them to peruse the rest of the book as well.

◆ If children like the cover and the blurb, they might read the first chapter as an "acid test" to decide whether they want to read the book. This is what Allen says he does. If he reads the first chapter and finds it exciting or intriguing, he's likely to check out—and maybe even buy—that book. But if the first chapter confuses him, with too many characters or too much going on—or too little—he'll unceremoniously slip it back on the shelf.

Allen says he also looks for early hints as to "how the characters talk," and also to see how difficult the book is. For instance, some children who start *The Yearling* by Marjorie Rawlings are initially put off by the heavy use of dialect. Many adults might remember being cowed by that same book, for the same reason. Here adults might give accomplished readers a nudge to see if they can get them past that first chapter. Books like *The Yearling* are worth a try, because many children enjoy them despite the added challenge of literary devices like dialect.

◆ If your child is joining the ranks of the avid readers, and she's beginning to trust your judgment, try gently pushing the tougher-to-crack books occasionally. (Though if your child is a noninterested reader, you're going to encounter lots of trouble—and perhaps even thwart your whole effort—by encouraging books that seem hard to approach from the get-go. For some better ideas, see Luring the Noninterested Reader and the Junk Book Junkie, p. 39.)

Here's where the school system might come to the rescue: eventually the tough "goodies" are going to appear on a vacation reading list in junior high or high school. You're going to have earned this help!

◆ Here's an open secret librarians and teachers are wise to: when asked, many children freely say they read certain books because the other kids are "reading" them. "Reading" means they are buying them and checking them out of libraries, but a good many children admit to not really reading them. These "status books" are most likely the popular fad series which are deemed "collectibles." A young girl mentioned in a *Horn Book Magazine* article described herself as an avid collector of Goosebumps books because everyone else was. But she reported she'd quit reading the books some time ago.

In fact, children frequently—if privately—complain that in many of the popular series books, the plots don't all make sense and that the writing is "not that good." But it's telling that even still, horror series guru R.L. Stine recently won Allen's elementary school's annual "Favorite Author" contest.

If a good number of the children who voted for R.L. Stine had been exposed to other work, perhaps those horror books would have been relegated to the "children's occasional guilty pleasure" category, not the heart of their reading lives. Were it not for parents who realize their children need to be more challenged in their reading, they would all be subsisting on the cheap books, and never finishing them, too. Now, *that's* scary.

A Story of Personal Inspiration

A great thing happened to Allen in the middle of second grade, when he was starting to ride the crest of the reading wave generated by our newly dubbed Magic Bookshelf. Allen befriended a boy in his class, John, who was such a prodigious reader that he was knocking out books like *The Swiss Family Robinson* and *Where the Red Fern Grows*.

Those were obviously tough reads for a then-eight-year-old. But aside from the marvelous model this new friend provided, we also became deeply impressed by Allen's simple respect for John. Though Allen is a bright child who does very well in school, the people he seemed to have the most respect for then were soccer coaches. That's fine too—and sports figures still hold their deserved share of Allen's admiration—but the fact that competitive Allen also looked up to one of his bookish peers enough to want to emulate him can, aside from the fact that John is a nice kid, be credited to Allen's realization that reading is a desirable and respectable activity, and that mastering it is something to be admired.

John went on to help Allen find new books, and they still recommend books to one another. Allen was pleased when he persuaded John to read *Charlie and the Chocolate Factory*. In the second half of second grade, the two signed up to be "reading buddies" in their classroom program, and decided to tackle the children's novels of E.B. White (advanced for their age, perhaps, but not in outer space). They have conversations about books at school, and it's clear Allen respects John's input and tries to impress him.

You might say: *but that's reading for the wrong reasons.* In some instances, that might well be. And we would be worried if we didn't see Allen freely reading on his own at our house, and enjoying what he reads. But just as he enjoys playing soccer, he is a fierce competitor. He hates to lose. Yet we feel his competitiveness is driven by the activity's importance to him. We suspect this is the same with his reading.

So, it's a delicate issue. John's advanced reading level seems to have been for the most part a good, strong influence. Allen knows John is a more advanced reader than he is, and seems to accept it gracefully. Every situation is different, so parents must weigh the factors surrounding their childrens' reading habits and keep looking for ways to encourage and praise their efforts, while eliminating all elements that discourage it.

Even with John's encouragement to read harder material, Allen usually sticks to his comfort zone, which is how it should be. His occasional voyages into loftier reading are seemingly taken with no more real seriousness than our own ambitious, yet doomed, childhood campaigns to read the entire dictionary.

Allen's reading buddy helped build the momentum created by our Magic Bookshelf. Reading worthwhile books was already part of Allen's world, but John helped solidify that part of Allen's self identity. And, perhaps, the competitive challenge moved both boys' reading up yet another notch.

We want to reinforce that children have plenty of time to

move on to the more advanced stuff. By next year, your child might have outgrown, say, the middle-grade science fiction tale *The White Mountains*, or the delightfully silly *Finn Family Moomintroll*. Balance high reading ability and ambition by simultaneously encouraging other reading that is comfortable. Like their fleeting babyhood, the phases of our children's lives are not frozen in time. They outgrow these stages quickly. Let them enjoy being children and reading books that were written for them.

A picture book, like a toy, invites participation. A mechanical toy may seem very clever to adults. But it is the toy and not the child that plays.
—Gail E. Haley, Caldecott-winning illustrator of A Story—A Story

Mixing Books With Other Media

We don't live in the Dark Ages, thank goodness. We can use other media to boost our children's reading programs. It doesn't take much to turn an ordinary activity, like taking your child and a friend to a movie, or watching a TV or video adaptation of a book, or putting in a computer CD-ROM, to turn that simple activity into one that integrates reading experience.

Technology may soon fulfill the promise it has held for so long when it comes to education. Computers and other multimedia devices can hold a child's attention in a way only television can match. But much of what is available in these formats is still text based, a boon to improving reading ability. And unlike the passive medium of TV, a computer almost cries out for interaction. You have to do something to get an action from the computer, and it is often far more engaging than simply clicking a remote control.

The synergy of children's books, with their colorful art and visual story lines, and computers gives us hope that a new tool is now available. While the schlock will inevitably be out there, some excellent children's books are now available in multimedia formats. Of particular interest is the Living Books series by

Learning to Make Comparisons

Not only can children be encouraged to compare and contrast books with other media, but they can compare books with other books. Introduce discussions about books by the same author, or books on similar subjects—for example, nature and animals (like the work of E.B. White, Wilson Rawls, and Marjorie Rawlings). It might not seem like it now—and it certainly doesn't have to be your primary intention—but this kind of discussion helps lay the groundwork for the unavoidable themes and comparative literature classes your children will face in high school and college. However, instead of setting up such exercises like drills, these casual but directed discussions require the child to stretch his mind, to consider the books and the elements in them carefully. He is learning not only to read the books, but to explore them and what they mean.

Broderbund Software. This software allows children to either read for themselves as they turn electronic pages or listen to an audio version that reads it for them. Children who enjoy these books can easily be talked into switching to paper versions of books by the same author. If you have a computer or access to one, consider this a potential tool to help your child.

Computers aren't the only tools available, however. The ideas below can help you put technology to work in your quest for good, meaningful literature.

◆ When there's a new movie based on a book your child has read, arrange to see or rent it if you deem it suitable for his age. Always first encourage him to read the book, just as many of us try to do as adults. Rarely are the adaptations of books to films, with some notable exceptions, better—than the books.

Also, keep in mind that a lot can happen between a book and a movie based on the same book. That many filmmakers sprinkle simple children's stories with profanity and raunchy situations appals many parents. The filmmakers probably do this to receive PG or PG-13 ratings, which they think are more appealing to the potential adult viewers, though it would seem that their not being content with a "G" often excludes much of the younger potential viewing audience.

◆ Invite discussion about the differences between the book and the movie. This is fun for the child, but adults often can have the added pleasure of hearing the child admit the book was better than the hyped-up film. Some examples are the early 1970s film *Willy Wonka and the Chocolate Factory,* which blanches in comparison to the book on which is was based, *Charlie and the Chocolate Factory*; *Matilda* (another adaptation from a book by Roald Dahl, who somehow always comes across as far more subversive on film than on paper); and *Harriet the Spy*, based on the book of the same name by Louise Fitzhugh. Some people may find the movies cute, but it's sad that many children think all there is of those clever classic stories are the so-so, one-dimensional movies.

Other rental movie ideas include *The Borrowers;* one of numerous movie versions of *Tom Sawyer; The Indian in the Cupboard*; *Little Women*; and *The Secret Garden.* There is no shortage to choose from. Some of these movies are quite good, such as the most recent remake of A *Little Princess*. Most movies, both for children and adults, are based on books—just check the movie credits. And typically, movie versions of books will spur new editions of the books with blurbs about the movie on the cover. Children will have fun comparing and contrasting movies and books, and at the same time they will be forging new links between reading and other enjoyable activities.

◆ Children's books are widely available on tape for playing in the car or other places. Dramatic readings by professional actor/readers can seem almost as good as being read to in person. Even better, with a little looking, you can find recordings of well-loved authors reading their own work, like T.S. Eliot reading his *Old Possum's Book of Practical Cats*, Dylan Thomas reading *A Child's Christmas in Wales*, and Carl Sandburg reading *Rootabaga Stories*. Also, most Newbery Award-winning books are available as dramatized recordings.

Surely we all remember the read-along records from our childhood. A beep signaled when we were to turn the page. And when we became "big kids," we graduated to the other side of the record, which deleted the cues. The same thing is available on tape and CD today. While no substitute for cozy reading aloud, these recordings can give your child the sensation of "reading along" to favorite books. Dr. Seuss classics are a particularly good choice, because of their liveliness and the fact that so many have been recorded. And more and more books for older children are becoming available on tape. Classics are usually available as books on tape because publishers feel safe with them. (See the appendix for information about audiobook companies and catalogs.)

◆ Some multimedia adaptations of children's books are now available on CD-ROM, if you use a computer at home. Try to encourage the reading of the book first, but certain software titles like Broderbund's version of *Arthur's Teacher Trouble* based on Marc Brown's book, are delightful. Unlike TV, these offer true interaction and cause-and-effect exercises. And they are mesmerizing.

Unlike computer games, interactive books allow children to explore objects, personalities, and storylines, with language—they can sometimes even alter storylines and create their own. Many of these also offer a choice of the child's reading the text silently or having the text "read aloud" by the program.

Research supports this type of multimedia learning, demonstrating that text being shown and read aloud is effective in boosting children's reading skills. Of course, nothing can substitute for the more old-fashioned scenarios of families reading together and children reading on their own. But according to *Electronic Learning* magazine, early research indicates that multimedia offers a whole new set of skills applicable to the world of today and the future, mainly the ability to integrate information from various formats at once. And, as many adults are well aware, computers can be vital tools in a household—not only for writing and editing, but for Internet research, corresponding by e-mail, balancing checkbooks and otherwise managing finances, for learning on CD-ROMs, and enjoying multimedia games, from canasta to Myst.

Parents interested in computers and software will enjoy researching and procuring good programs for their children. Children's software is big business, and new software is reviewed and described in magazines such as *Home PC, Family Computing,* and *Mac Home Journal.* You can also look for computer programs and CD-ROMs that address specific topics your children enjoy learning about.

◆ Introducing "good books" in multimedia format is a magnificent way to lure in noninterested readers as well. They offer yet another way to expose such a child to good writing and clever ideas.

"Hip" kids might be surprised and impressed to realize popular music like rap consists not only of steady rhythm and musical arrangements, but songs—or "raps"—in rhyme. Some classroom experiments have sparked children's interest in poetry. After all, it does take a flair for rhyme and writing to compose and perform this music. As Sue McLeaf Nespeca pointed out in her May 1996 *School Library Journal* article "Literacy Begins at Home: 25 Ways to Make Sure Reading Runs in the Family," a surprising number of children's poems and books can be rapped. Examples include *Crocodile Beat* by Gail Jorgenson; *Bein' With You This Way* by W. Nikola-Lisa; and *1, 2, Buckle My Shoe* by Liz Loveless.

◆ Lots of children's book and reading resources can be discovered on the Internet. You can find some listed on p. 52 in the chapter The Bond Between Reading and Writing and in the appendix with more parents' resources. At least one Internet site, the Jolly Roger, even offers a complete library of classics, with original illustrations (jollyroger.com/treasureisland.html). This seems an interesting juxtaposition of things: old-fashioned, time-honored literature in a cutting-edge medium—and proof that the classics endure, even in cyber-space.

◆ You might collect various magazines, newspapers, and newsletters in your home. When you see an article or item that would interest your child, pull it out and give it to her. Children hear snippets of news from TV, radio, and personal conversations; reading something about current issues can enhance understanding, clear up misconceptions, and broaden their knowledge of the world.

There are only two lasting bequests we can hope to give our children. One is roots; the other, wings.
—From Mothers & Babies: The Perfect Love, *published by Great Quotations, Inc. Lombard, Illinois*

If Your Child Does Not Live With You

If your child does not live with you—whether you're a parent without full-time custody, a grandparent or other relative, or even a family friend—you can still build and maintain a Magic Bookshelf in your own home, as long as the child is a regular visitor. (And if she doesn't regularly spend time at your home, you can work on stocking one in the home where she does spend the most time.)

As always, reading begins with modeling behavior. The temptation is great to be the "Party Dad" or Mom, or the indulgent grandparents, or doting aunt or uncle who always takes the children where they seem to most want to go—the zoo, the pizza parlor, the movies, and so on. While such activities can be important, so is introducing children to experiences that will expand their minds, ignite their imaginations, and help mold them into well-rounded and thoughtful people.

And remember, children pay much more attention to what you *do* than to what you *say*. Consider the following suggestions to make a part-time home a reading haven:

◆ Give books a prominent place in your own home. Stock bookshelves well, and keep books within easy reach, such as on coffee tables and nightstands. (See Nurturing the Reading Habit Naturally, p. 17.)

◆ Instead of always going to the park, make trips to the library a regular outing. Get the child his own card at your local library as soon as possible, and make a big deal out of it. Keep the card at your house for him, which makes it seem a special privilege and may even encourage him to suggest trips to the library on his own. (See In Celebration of the Library Card, p. 26.)

Make the library an integral part of your time with the child. For example, outline activities by saying, "Let's go to your soccer game and then head to the library." When you so naturally make it part of the day, you're likely to have few complaints.

◆ The next time there's birthday money to be spent, suggest shopping at a bookstore instead of a toy store. Also, remember gift certificates to bookstores make great presents and give you some control over what the child buys. But first make the bookstore an attractive place by letting the child know you often go there yourself.

◆ Buy books frequently. Many are inexpensive and make nice little "hello" presents aside from birthdays, Christmas, and other occasions. For children who visit less often, consider making trips to a bookstore for an inexpensive paperback a part of your routine. Some stores even have clubs children can join and earn points toward a T-shirt or some other prize with each purchase.

◆ Read aloud together. There's no better opportunity to share one-on-one moments. Spend those last precious minutes of the day relaxing, reading a book that is a mutual favorite. Also, keep a good book of short stories for when the child visits to provide reading that can be finished in one sitting.

◆ For children who visit frequently, maintain a longer book in progress at your house. This is always handy when those inevitable moments of boredom strike, but it also establishes continuity to visits. You might also set up a reading niche for the child, as described in Nurturing the Reading Habit, Naturally (p. 17).

The list at the back of this book offers some ideas for where to start in buying or borrowing books. The library is an especially good choice here because it allows you and the child to test drive some topics and authors and explore what might become favorite reading material. For school-age children, consider making a call to the child's teacher or school librarian to discuss reading interests and ability, and get some better ideas of what to try.

◆ If the child visits frequently, encourage her to keep a book she's reading on a desk or beside her bed at your house—especially if it's a nice book you don't want to get banged around in a bookbag. If it's a paperback or a book not intended solely for the "home library" at your place, let her carry it around to read wherever she is. Non-custodial parents and relatives know how hard it can be for a child to keep up with things that move from home to home. These days, children get around more than ever—to school, to afterschool programs, to sports practice, and to friends' homes, not to mention "second homes."

Make Your Time Together Count

Even if the child lives far away or visits are otherwise rare, try to stock a Magic Bookshelf remotely. Keep special books at your house and try to monitor the child's progress and likes and dislikes, such as with meal-time discussions about books. But also furnish him with books to take back to his permanent home, since he's there most.

Parents and others who rely on short visitation times with children seek to make the visits special. They try to make up for lost time, striving to forge, maintain, and strengthen bonds. There's no better way to do this than with books—reading aloud and sharing experiences that involve everyone. This sidesteps much of the intricate planning and constant money spending and theme park-hopping that many weekend families end up resorting to. Spending time on reading and sharing beats the guilty feeling of overcompensation from going to the toy store all the time. Moreover, most of us remember happy experiences and simple times more than material things.

You can't buy time with your children, but you can invest what you get wisely. Read to them. Hold them in your lap and let them turn the pages and even read a few passages for themselves. Believe us: these times build much stronger bonds than a few roller-coaster rides.

I recommend what I call sure-fire books at first.
— Irene Hunt, author of the Newbery Award-winning novel
Up A Road Slowly

How to Use This List

This is a comprehensive working list of selected picture books, short story collections, juvenile novels, and nonfiction and poetry books that together should provide a solid starting place in finding good, well-rounded literary choices for children. (More lists on p. 43 suggest alternatives to popular but disposable series and genre books.)

These lists should serve as jump-off points—when a book is a "hit," try moving on to others by the same author, or seek titles that address similar topics or themes. Or, go on to books that feature similar characters or that share similar historical backdrops.

An additional feature is that many of the books on this list, from picture books to novels, have developed into series, the kind that have come about not by marketing device but which sprang from a colorful cast of characters who just had more to do. We've indicated where books have sequels or whole series behind them.

We've sought variety in our suggestions. We've also tried to stick mostly with the hits. Many of our choices have reached, or nearly reached, the status of modern classics because of their enormous popularity with children, not just with librarians and teachers. However, we've included certain classics—such as *Alice's*

Adventures in Wonderland and *The Adventures of Robin Hood*—that we think should be attempted, even if it takes some parental help, because of their cultural literacy factor as well as their fantastic stories. These books contain characters and situations that children will hear referred to over and over throughout their entire lives. When a child hears the expressions "grinning like a Cheshire cat," or "robbing from the rich to give to the poor," she'll know right where they came from, and this is important.

Other books are on the list for purely aesthetic purposes—for the sheer beauty of the writing and language—as well as the great stories. But though the books we've chosen are meant to be challenging, most people wouldn't consider them "highbrow."

We want our children to *use* their reading skills. Musicians seek to do more than just play scales. Likewise, these books help your child do more than simply fill in boxes on reading skill cards. While some books do nudge children to flex reading abilities like mastering more difficult words, bear in mind reading is more than a drill. Books can challenge children to think even when the words themselves aren't difficult. You can help engage the thought process by asking casual follow-up questions to see what your child thinks the material means. Was what happened expected? Could it have been? To prove how accessible books are that prompt these sorts of questions, consider *The Cat in the Hat!*

From *Curious George* to *Charlotte's Web*, books can help a child learn to anticipate and analyze what happens. Most of the books on this list, regardless of genre, reveal lessons learned about others and ourselves. Complex novels like *Where the Red Fern Grows, A Girl Named Disaster*, and *Jacob Have I Loved* (the latter from the Newbery awards list) prompt children to think back and then piece it all together—as is essential in real life.

Time-testing has shown the books on this list to be loved and respected by legions of children. Though fine books have been produced in recent years, and indeed continue to be, most of the books on our list are ten years old or more—often much more. You'll need to use your child's interests and abilities as a yardstick to pick out the right ones, and apply that insight as well to other books, including the new ones coming out constantly.

However, to help you "nail a few" according to a child's preferences, we've grouped the novels by genre: fantasy; mystery/ scary; sci-fi/adventure; growing-up themes; everyday kids; and animals (although as you will see, most books could fall neatly into two or even three different categories).

One more feature of this list: the best test of whether a book will fit the reading and interest levels of a child—other than the child himself—is a parent's or other knowing adult's discerning eye. So we've noted where novels and nonfiction are for early grade readers (like chapter books), or for more advanced readers; or whether picture books are intended for babies, preschoolers or beginning readers; and so forth. This might help cut down on your time at first. But once you get started, you'll find your own— and your child's—noses leading you to the right place time after time. And this knack will serve you better than any list!

Lastly, there are many, many other books that could and should have been included on this list, if it were humanly possible to know about every good book written and about all the good books in progress, and if we'd had hundreds of extra pages to fill. Also, nothing can substitute for personal taste. Use this list as your departure point into your child's flights of literary fancy. But always keep in mind that journeys of the mind make many unexpected stops. Let our list serve not as a road map but simply as a travel guide to consult from your armchair before the journey begins.

Picture Books and Easy Readers

Allard, Harry. *Miss Nelson Is Missing!* Illustrated by James Marshall. Miss Nelson is so nice and kind her class starts taking advantage of her. Enter the wicked substitute, Miss Viola Swamp. Herein lies a gentle moral about showing due appreciation for the good things—and people—in life. There are two sequels to this book, *Miss Nelson Is Back* and *Miss Nelson Has a Field Day*.

Barrett, Judi. *Cloudy With a Chance of Meatballs.* Illustrated by Ron Barrett. The people of Chewandswallow sure have it good, with weather that comes down in the form of food … spaghetti and meatballs, scrambled eggs and toast, even hamburgers. Until the weather takes an ugly turn for the worse. Children will laugh out loud at this absurd and wonderful tale, as imaginatively illustrated as it is told.

Base, Graeme. *The Eleventh Hour.* When Horace the elephant turns eleven, he invites his animal friends over for a splendid party. But then a curious mystery emerges. This gorgeously illustrated novelty book requires some concentration and smarts on the part of the reader. Look for other books by Base including *The Discovery of Dragons* and *Animalia*.

Bemelmans, Ludwig. *Madeline.* One of the sequels to this well-known book, *Madeline's Rescue*, won a Caldecott award in 1954. All center on the delightful adventures of plucky Madeline, a resident of a well-run French orphanage where little girls live "in two straight lines," guided by sweet Miss Clavel. Many incarnations of these books can be found in bookstores today, with videos, Madeline play sets with cloth dolls and trousseaus, and paper dolls and such. **SERIES.**

Brown, Margaret Wise. *Big Red Barn*. Illustrated by Felicia Bond. Animals are the only characters in this sweet, rhyming story about a day on a farm, and how all the animals sleepily turn in for the night. The drawings will intrigue young children, who will insist on accounting for all the animals—and counting the eggs in the clutch—every time. **BABIES AND TODDLERS.**

Note: Many parents are already familiar with Wise's toddler classic *Goodnight Moon*, illustrated by Clement Thacher Hurd. Both of these must-haves are available in durable and totable board book editions.

Carle, Eric. *The Very Hungry Caterpillar.* A tiny caterpillar with a giant appetite evolves into a butterfly after it eats various pieces of fruit and other good things. This is a hands-on board book designed just for babies and toddlers to handle and chew. Thus, it's definitely one to own. **BABIES AND TODDLERS.**

Carlstrom, Nancy White. *Blow Me a Kiss, Miss Lilly.* Illustrated by Amy Schwartz. Sweet story of a little girl's friendship with the elderly, life-embracing Miss Lilly, and how the girl keeps Miss Lilly's memory alive after she dies. This book offers perspective and lessons on coping with loss, while cherishing memories. A good book for a child who has lost a relative or friend to illness or death.

Note: A very different book by Carlstrom is the clever *Jesse Bear, What Will You Wear?*, a well-established toddler fave.

Day, Alexandra. *Good Dog, Carl.* A big, friendly Rottweiler is frequently charged with caring for a baby. Virtually a picture-only book, with lovely paintings and lively stories about the pair's adventures. It's also subversive in a way that makes parents crack a smile instead of a frown: what mother would leave her baby in a park with a dog? Then again, how many people have Carl for a dog? Other Carl books include *Carl's Afternoon in the Park, Carl's Masquerade*, and *Carl Goes Shopping.* **BABIES AND TODDLERS. SERIES.**

Degen, Bruce. *Jamberry.* A joyous rhyming romp through the berry patches with a boy and a bear. The exuberant illustrations, bursting with color, grow more delightful with each perusal, as smaller details emerge. The large-print, spare text in this extremely popular book melds perfectly with the pictures, and shows that so-called "nonsense rhyme" can be the most special of all. **TODDLERS AND PRESCHOOLERS.**

DePaola, Tomie. *Strega Nona*. Villager Strega Nona knows magical spells for making never-ending pots of spaghetti. But when a nosy visitor tries to steal the spell and work the magic for himself, he soon sees the folly of his ways—and the reader sees the fun in it, as well as the severe consequences. The come-uppance of the underhanded spell-stealer is particularly satisfying. Other Strega Nona books include *Merry Christmas, Strega Nona.*

duBois, William Pène. *Lion*. Challenging, fun book for transitional readers, with wonderful pictures. Also great to read aloud. This is a quaint, delightfully dated book about an angel named Foreman who creates the Lion, king of beasts, after a number of hilarious, unsuccessful tries. Your child is sure to giggle at the angel's early lion prototypes. Published in 1956 and now out of print, this book is a library staple for you to check out again and again.

Friedman, Ina. *How My Parents Learned To Eat*. Illustrated by Allan Say. An American sailor is afraid to ask a Japanese schoolgirl to dinner—he doesn't know how to use chopsticks. Meanwhile, she's worried because she doesn't know how to use a knife and fork. So they each secretly learn to eat the other's way, and end up meeting in the middle. This humorous and charming book, told from the point of view of their culturally ambidextrous daughter, is as much about bridging cultural gaps as it is about dealing with the universal frustrations of table manners.

Havill, Juanita. *Jamaica Tag-Along*. Illustrated by Anne Sibley O'Brien. Jamaica wants to play ball with her older brother Ossie, who clearly does not want her tagging along. But the shoe is on the other foot when little Berto wants to play with *her*. A realistic story with a nice message.

Heyward, DuBose. *The Country Bunny and the Little Gold Shoes*. Illustrated by Marjorie Flack. All the Easter bunnies in the past have been white, male rabbits, but when a brown female bunny mother gets her turn, she fills the shoes like no other. The moral implications of this 1940s-era book are obvious, but the message is noble and the comparatively long story is quite absorbing for a picture book. Though some critics have questioned why this book has enormous appeal to children, the fact that it remains a bestseller speaks volumes. And the "retro" pastel pictures are charming.

Hoban, Russell. *Bread and Jam for Frances*. Illustrated by Lillian Hoban. Little badger Frances eschews all food, no matter how attractive it is to the rest of the family, and sticks with her favorite bread and jam. With bread and jam, she explains, "I always know what I am getting, and I am always pleased." Mother and Father prompt a turnaround by giving Frances only what she likes—bread and jam, morning, noon and night. Hoban's Frances series (including *Bedtime for Frances* and *A Baby Sister for Frances*) is so well-loved and enduring not only because it is amusing, but because it mirrors the thoughts and behavior of real, intelligent children. Beginning readers can graduate to *A Bargain for Frances*. **SERIES.**

Johnson, Angela. *When I Am Old With You*. Illustrated by David Soman. Beautiful story and pictures to match about an African-American girl who imagines herself growing old with her grandfather, and muses about what they will do together in their old age. Warning: Parents must brace themselves for this poignant glimpse inside a child's worldview.

Jorgensen, Gail. *Crocodile Beat*. Illustrated by Patricia Mullins. Rhythmic jungle tale about a hungry crocodile and the brave lion that protects the jungle creatures. This book is listed in our section about mixing books and other media, because it can so effectively be rapped. See if you can put the rhythm in your tot. **BABIES AND TODDLERS.**

Keats, Ezra Jack. *Peter's Chair*. This 1967 book about a little boy coming to terms with a new baby sister features some slightly old-fashioned references to boys having blue things and girls having pink. But this is a sweet, often recommended story of an African-American family. **PRESCHOOLERS.**

Kuskin, Karla. *The Philharmonic Gets Dressed*. Illustrated by Marc Simont. It's Friday night, and ninety-two men and thirteen women, all musicians in the Philharmonic orchestra, are getting ready for work. This simple telling shows in humorously precise detail how they use their own personal styles to bathe, dress in formal wear, say goodbye to their families, and get to Philharmonic Hall on time. It also delivers a sense of anticipation and excitement about the important job of making beautiful music.

MacLachlan, Patricia. *All the Places To Love*. Illustrated by Mike Wimmer. This is the touching story of a boy whose rural family shows him "all the places to love." The text is accompanied by realistic, affecting paintings that are likely to prompt a few tears from the adult reader. This book simply and eloquently portrays how one's home and family are the essence of life.

Martin, Bill Jr., and John Archambault. *Barn Dance!* Illustrated by Ted Rand. With its knee-slapping rhythm and perfect use of country dialect, this warm and rousing tale of a curious boy who is magically drawn to a farm animals' midnight barn dance is the closest thing to music we've ever seen on a printed page. Written to be read aloud (it has been featured on the PBS children's series Reading Rainbow), this captivating book enchants children and adults alike.

Mosel, Arlene. *Tikki Tikki Tembo*. Illustrated by Blair Lent. Why Chinese children should have short names. This book seems to appear on almost every book list you consult. Published in the late 1960s, this poignant and to-the-point story, accompanied by memorable blue and black illustrations, has become *the* classic retelling of a Chinese folktale.

Parish, Peggy. *Amelia Bedelia*. Illustrated by Fritz Siebel. Amelia Bedelia is a well-meaning, good-hearted woman who needs a job. She finally gets a seemingly suitable one, as a housekeeper. But her literal, childlike mind interprets simple directions like "dressing the chicken" and "dusting the furniture" to disastrous and hilarious effect. Fortunately for Amelia Bedelia, she's a terrific baker of sweets, a talent that always saves her—and her job—in the end. Amelia teaches children to look at things in a new light, and gives those old enough to get the puns a marvelous sense of what language really is—a way to communicate. **SERIES.**

Peet, Bill. *The Whingdingdilly*. Scamp the farm dog suffers from a common affliction: he wishes he were something else, something flashier. That is, until an impish witch grants his wish, and turns him into the dreaded and exotic Whingdingdilly. When he is captured and miserably displayed in C.J. Pringle's Palace of Living Wonders, he realizes he's had the good life all along. Luckily for him, he's mercifully returned to his former status, and to his loving owner, Orvie Jarvis.

Note: Peet fans—and there are scads—rejoice that he is so prolific. His books sometimes are even relegated to special Peet sections on library shelves. Further, fans should not miss his excellent *Bill Peet: An Autobiography* for middle grade and young adult readers, which is described in the nonfiction section.

Pinkwater, Daniel M. *Tooth-Gnasher Superflash*. Sometimes dry, always madcap humor characterizes Pinkwater's books, which show an uncommon respect for children's thoughts and ways, and an amusing raised-eyebrow regard for the world of adults. In this one, Mr. and Mrs. Popsnorkle and the five little Popsnorkles are wowed when they test-drive the fantastic Tooth-Gnasher Superflash, a car that does amazing things (like turning into a dinosaur and running on its hind legs). Parents enjoy the prolific Pinkwater as much as children do. Also look for *Author's Day* and *Guys From Space*.

Note: A testament to Pinkwater's popularity is how south Georgia writer Bailey White became a fellow commentator on the National Public Radio program *All Things Considered*, and later a well-respected author. White met Pinkwater after her first-grade students, rabid Pinkwater fans, wrote him a fan letter and thus initiated a correspondence.

Potter, Beatrix. *The Tale of Peter Rabbit*. Once you get past the mass-market Peter Rabbit dolls, plates, toys, and other items, you have a sweet story that never loses its appeal. Beatrix Potter's classic tale of a mischievous rabbit and his siblings teaches, scolds, and entertains children of any generation. No bookshelf in a young child's room can produce true magic without a well-worn copy of a Peter Rabbit book. **SERIES.**

Rey, H.A. *Curious George*. All the wonderful stories of the famously curious little monkey who continually gets into mischief when his guardian, the Man in the Yellow Hat, steps away. These books help children learn to anticipate the inevitable consequences of actions taken by the characters in the stories. **SERIES.**

Scarry, Richard. *Best Word Book Ever*. Put a child's nose into one of Scarry's generously sized books, and it likely will not emerge for a long while. Every page is "peopled" with inventive and colorful animal characters and corresponding situations. It's not uncommon for a child to spend fifteen minutes on one page. Children are fascinated by the books' hectic goings-on and all the tiny details. Practically every reading—or extended viewing—yields a new discovery or joke. Also look for Richard Scarry's *Busy, Busy World*; and *Cars and Trucks and Things That Go*. **TODDLERS AND PRESCHOOLERS.**

Schuett, Stacey. *Somewhere in the World Right Now*. This relatively new book adds depth to a child's worldview—it wraps a geography lesson and a study of time zone differences around a cozy bedtime story. In pretty prose and rich, lush pictures superimposed over maps, we see how people—and animals—around the wide world tend to their own personal routines, in the very same moments. African elephants sway from side to side as they sleep standing up, while Himalayan farmers tend their crops, and a child goes to bed in Massachusetts.

Seuss, Dr. *The Cat in the Hat; One Fish, Two Fish, Red Fish, Blue Fish*. What is there to say? Childhood without a generous stack of Seuss tales—these and all the others—would seem empty. Sing-song rhymes and unforgettable characters make these books a first step to reading that few children can resist. The easy-to-remember tales can have children "reading" the book to you—after about a hundred readings by you. In *The Cat in the Hat*, Mother is out on a cold, cold wet day ... and a colorful cat with some wild antics up his sleeve shows up and helps create mayhem. Most Seuss books are available on tape so children can "read along" in the car or in their rooms by turning pages when a beep signals them to do so. **EARLY READERS.**

Shaw, Nancy. *Sheep in a Jeep*. Illustrated by Margot Apple. Funny, infectious sing-song tale of a bunch of adventurous sheep who take an ill-fated jaunt in a jeep. You must have this giddy romp on your shelf, and look for others including *Sheep in a Shop*. **PRESCHOOLERS; EARLY READERS.**

Sis, Peter. *The Three Golden Keys*. Haunting and beautiful autobiographical story Sis wrote and illustrated for his daughter Madeleine about his memories of Prague, where he grew up. A hot-air balloonist lands in an ancient city, which he soon realizes is his childhood home, preserved just as he left it. However, he finds that in order to unlock and enter the house where he spent his boyhood, he must collect three golden keys. To win them he must follow a black cat to special places of his childhood and recall Czech legends from his youth. Adults will be moved by the sentimental and nostalgic story, and children will be captivated by its dream-like spell.

Skorpen, Liesel Moak. *We Were Tired of Living in a House*. Illustrated by Doris Burn. Every child at some point or other fantasizes about running off with a suitcase and a bedroll to sample life on his or her own. In this charming book, a band of four small children, all tired of living in a house, try out life in a tree, in a cave, on a pond, and at the sea shore. Of course, they like these new digs, but there's always just a little something that is not quite right. Simple, poetic writing and delightful pictures.

Steig, William. *Doctor De Soto*. Dr. De Soto and his wife must find a way to provide dental work for a hungry fox who rudely plans to eat them with his newly repaired teeth. True lessons about life can be learned from the couple who finish the job while creatively meeting an intimidating challenge.

Thompson, Kay. *Eloise*. Illustrated by Hilary Knight. The "sophisticated" 1950s classic about quintessential only child Eloise, who lives at The Plaza with Nanny, Weenie her dog, and Skipperdee her turtle, and bides her time challenging her fellow hotel dwellers. Fortunately, more children tend to laugh at, rather than emulate, the often bratty antics of Eloise. These books also are delightfully illustrated and the text creatively arranged to float around the pages. Adults often fiercely guard these books as parts of their private collections. Also keep a lookout for the rare, out-of-print *Eloise at Christmastime* and *Eloise in Paris*.

Viorst, Judith. *Alexander and the Terrible, Horrible, No Good, Very Bad Day*. Illustrated by Ray Cruz. Alexander's day is unspeakably awful from the moment he gets up to the time he goes to bed. We can all relate—so can children, who will take comfort in knowing other people have such days too.

Real Mother Goose, The. Illustrated by Blanche Fisher Wright. Traditional nursery rhymes for infants and up. This is the edition you—and your parents too—might remember from your own childhoods. Parents can also find many other fine Mother Goose anthologies, including *Tomie dePaola's Mother Goose*. **BABIES AND UP.**

Books of Short Stories

Garis, Howard R. *Uncle Wiggily's Story Book*. Circa 1920s classic tales about one of the most enduring storybook characters in American literature, Uncle Wiggily, "the cheerful bunny rabbit gentleman," who along with Nurse Jane Fuzzy Wuzzy and friends is always available to help those in need, from children who have toothaches or have fallen in mud puddles to Santa Claus himself.

Kipling, Rudyard. *Just So Stories*. These elegant fables, circa 1912—such as "The Elephant's Child" and "How the Leopard Got His Spots"—seem as integral to childhood as playing catch or skipping rope. A volume of these stories belongs on every Magic Bookshelf. You simply can't find finer writing for children. The natural companion to this collection is *The Jungle Book*.

Milne, A.A. *Winnie-the-Pooh*. Illustrated by Ernest Shepard. Charming tales about boy Christopher Robin and his friends from the Hundred-Acre Wood: self-deprecating Pooh, who classifies himself as "a bear of very little brain"; perky Piglet; pessimistic Eeyore; and the rest of the company. Pooh commercialism is so prevalent that it is easy to forget the clever and endearing humor that characterize these books. **SERIES.**

Sachar, Louis. *Sideways Stories from Wayside School*. Hilariously subversive stories about a zany school—not to mention its students and faculty—and their extremely, um, interesting school days, divided into easily digestible pieces. Wayside School stories are good for children who have trouble completing longer books. They can get a feeling of accomplishment and also may find themselves reading an entire book in little bites. And, of course, the stories do feature laugh-out-load scenes that are sure to please. Also look for *Wayside School is Falling Down*, and *Wayside School Gets a Little Stranger*. **EARLY GRADES.**

Sandburg, Carl. *Rootabaga Stories*. Can be found in one anthology or in two separate volumes, I and II. This is quintessential bedtime reading—stories like "How They Bring Back the Village of Cream Puffs When the Wind Blows It Away" and "The Wedding Procession of the Rag Doll and the Broom Handle and Who Was in It" are not only terrific tales but joyful celebrations of childhood by a master writer and storyteller.

Novels
(for middle grades, except where noted as early grade or advanced selections)

Fantasy

Alexander, Lloyd. The five *Prydain Chronicles*—*The Book of Three*; *The Black Cauldron*; *The Castle of Llyr*; *Taran Wanderer*; and *The High King* (which won the Newbery Award in 1969). A blend of mythology and Welsh legend, Alexander's finely written and completely absorbing books take place in the imaginary kingdom of Prydain, and describe the exciting adventures and great battles between good and evil. Central characters include Taran, an assistant pig-keeper and would-be hero, and Princess Eilonwy, a heroine who must learn to be a lady. **SERIES.**

Note: For younger readers, look for the Prydain picture books, illustrated by Evaline Ness. (Also see Alexander's middle-grade book *The Jedera Adventure* under SciFi/Adventure.)

Babbitt, Natalie. *Tuck Everlasting.* Instead of running away as she intends, sheltered Winnie Foster is kidnapped in the woods by a strange family—the rustic Tucks, whose members have eerily remained the same age for eighty-seven years after having drunk from an enchanted spring. Through this dreamy story—which escalates in the second half with a sinister spy, a murder, and a jailbreak—runs the theme of the "wheel of life." The Tucks, alas, have fallen off the wheel. In the end, Winnie must choose between joining the Tucks and their timeless cul-de-sac, or following the natural order of things. It is a poignant choice she makes.

Banks, Lynne. *The Indian in the Cupboard.* Illustrated by Brock Cole. The plastic Indian that Omri's brother gives him for his birthday at first seems a second-rate afterthought of a gift. But when Omri unlocks an old cupboard with a magical key, and then shuts the Indian inside, the toy comes alive. This beautiful tale goes deeper than just the entertaining over-story. It transcends the often cliched storylines of other tales about toys that come to life. This book examines the moral implications and dilemmas—not to mention the physical challenges—of being responsible for miniature, breathing beings. This book has several sequels, including *Return of the Indian* and *Secret of the Indian*. **SERIES.**

Baum, Frank L. *The Wizard of Oz.* Original illustrations by W. W. Denslow. Many more people have seen the Hollywood movie than have read the book about Kansas farm girl Dorothy and the friends she meets on the road to Oz. Splendid as it is, the movie doesn't have the fresh, simple charm of the book, which packs even more magic: for example, a Golden Cap; Silver Shoes instead of ruby slippers; the familiar Winged Monkeys, but with a good side; and many more fantastic and clever adventures. This is a grand read-aloud choice; children will enjoy looking over your shoulder at the plentiful pictures as you read. Best of all, many sequels follow. **SERIES.**

Note: Literary critics point out that Baum actually created an early feminist work by so empowering a little girl (younger in the book than Judy Garland's Dorothy) to lead a pack of adventurers seeking the services of the great Wizard of Oz. (Dorothy has herself owned the power to get home all along.) Critics also have noted many elements of this "fantasy" book are actually symbolic of the Industrial Revolution, when farmers began to suffer, and industrial cities (like the Emerald City) began to thrive. Looking at it this way, the descriptions of the Emerald City are especially amusing: everyone must wear green spectacles, presumably to cut the blinding glare of all that emerald. But in reality, the glasses just color everything green!

Carroll, Lewis. *Alice's Adventures in Wonderland.* The Victorian classic about the strange characters and situations proper young Alice encounters in Wonderland after an unexpected plunge down a rabbit hole. Most versions are accompanied by the cerebral sequel *Through the Looking Glass*. **ADVANCED READERS AND READ-ALOUD.**

Note: Pulitzer Prize-winning author Frank McCourt has said, "You could spend the rest of your life digging around in *Alice in Wonderland*." Parents should first read an annotated version of this book—such as *The Annotated Alice* with notes by Martin Gardner. Not only will it clarify the inside jokes, satiric twists on Victorian "pop culture," and the logic behind the brilliantly illogical situations, it will likely make you laugh out loud. A truly well-read person should know Alice, and it is far better to read Carroll's original than to depend on the often-watered down Alice of "whittled-down" versions and animated features. It is true that for some children, the book does have some nightmarish qualities, and the original illustrations by Sir John Tenniel can seem creepy. Consider reserving this book for junior high-age children, or reading it aloud and explaining some Victorian-era "jokes" along the way, which children might appreciate along with the silly situations. It can be worth the work.

Cooper, Susan. *The Dark Is Rising*. Illustrated by Alan E. Cober. Children battle the evil forces of the Dark in this riveting and elegantly written fantasy, through which the author weaves ancient Celtic and English traditions. Eleven-year-old Will, a member of a large village family, embarks on a century-transcending quest for six magical signs that will aid him and other chosen people in the battle between light and darkness. This book is the second in a five-part series, the first of which is *Over Sea, Under Stone*. The fourth book in the series, *The Grey King*, won a Newbery medal. **SERIES.**

Dahl, Roald. *Charlie and the Chocolate Factory*. Illustrated by Joseph Schindelman. Charlie Bucket, the only child in a poverty-stricken extended family, wants nothing more than to be one of the six lucky children who find a golden ticket in a chocolate bar, a find that will enable the winners to enter the most wonderful candy factory imaginable. And amazingly, Charlie wins. So he and the five other winners, spoiled children of desperately over-indulgent parents, visit the factory operated by the off-the-wall and utterly irreverent Willy Wonka—with scattered results. Charlie is an endearing character who teaches the benefits of virtue and sacrifice. No child can resist pulling for him as Dahl matches him against some insufferable children. The morals here are clearly stated. This book has a sequel, *Charlie and the Great Glass Elevator*.

Note: This is prime evidence that reading can be fun. Your children likely will need little prompting, but this book is often the gateway to Dahl's appealing array of children's classics such as *Danny, the Champion of the World* and *James and the Giant Peach* (the latter tops read-aloud guru Jim Trelease's list of the best read-aloud books around). In turn, these memorable books can and do serve as the hook to reading better literature.

de Sainte-Exupery, Antoine. *The Little Prince*. A lovely fable for children and adults about what is and is not important in life—hence the famous quote from the book: "What is essential is invisible to the eye." This is a "lifetime book"—most people receive it as children, then read it several times throughout their lives because of the perspective it provides.

Eager, Edward. *Half Magic*. Illustrated by N. M. Bodecker. There's no better escape during a summer or other vacation than the enchanting books of Edward Eager. In this one, four children trying to while away *their* boring summer vacation come upon what appears to be an ordinary nickel, but which turns out to be a magical coin that makes everything they wish come true—by half. Needless to say, the results are interesting. These circa 1950s books are truly timeless—Eager's stories often whisk the reader to other times and places anyway. Other Eager books include *Seven-Day Magic, Magic or Not?*, and *Knight's Castle*. **SERIES.**

Juster, Norton. *The Phantom Tollbooth*. Illustrated by Jules Feiffer. Protagonist Milo can't quite get interested in anything, the world around him being so very dull—until a mysterious box arrives one day, containing a toy tollbooth. Milo yawns, gets in his toy car, and drives it through the tollbooth, entering a magical and thoroughly entertaining world of words and numbers whose sides are at extreme odds with one another. For all to be righted, Milo must rescue the banished princesses Rhyme and Reason so sense and sanity can be restored to this disjointed world. Milo learns important lessons about learning and knowledge, and how they can overcome some seemingly insurmountable obstacles. He also sees what loyalty means through his learned guide—a dog named Tock. Adults will appreciate the author's clever blend of imagination and wordplay.

Lewis, C.S. *The Lion, The Witch And The Wardrobe.* The first book in the seven-volume Chronicles of Narnia. In this symbolism-rich classic, Lucy and her brothers and sister enter a magic wardrobe that serves as a door to Narnia, an icy, enchanted land in need of a savior—the mighty and noble lion Aslan—to break the evil spell cast by the White Witch. What Lewis has actually done is superimpose this entertaining and intense story over the basic message of Christianity. Discovering and interpreting the symbolism is a favorite pastime for many scholars—and for children and their parents. **SERIES.**

Nesbit, E. *The Enchanted Castle.* Illustrated by Paul O. Zelinsky. Gerald, Kathleen, and Jimmy embark on magical adventures when they stumble into a wonderful garden, befriend Mabel, and go on to discover an enchanted castle together. Written at the turn of the twentieth century, British author Nesbit's books still stir childrens' yearnings to escape from everyday life. After reading *The Enchanted Castle*, young readers will likely keep one eye trained for evidence of the unusual, hoping they too will find entrée into a magical world. Also look for other popular books by Nesbit, including *Five Children and It,* and *The Railway Children* (not to be confused with *The Boxcar Children*).

Note: Many young Nesbit fans *and adults* also love L.M. Boston's Green Knowe series, beginning with *The Children of Green Knowe*, in which children of the past come back to play with a lonely boy in a wonderful, magical old house. Consistently acclaimed for their fine writing and seamless blend of fantasy and realism, these novels are interwoven with stories of other periods in history.

Norton, Mary. *The Borrowers*. Illustrated by Beth and Joe Krush. The Borrowers are tiny people who "borrow" household items to maintain their miniature apartment, whose entrance lies under a grandfather clock in a spacious English country house. It's a wonder to see what the resourceful Borrowers have come up with to furnish their home—daughter Arrietty's fancy cigar box bedroom, mother Homily's thimble cooking pot, and the postage-stamp portraits that adorn the sitting room are just a few examples. What lends edge to this fantasy is the omnipresent threat of discovery by the giant humans. For a Borrower's greatest fear is that of being "seen." Other Borrower books include *The Borrowers Aloft* and *The Borrowers Afield*. **SERIES.**

Tolkien, J.R.R. *The Hobbit*. Shy, retiring Bilbo Baggins, thought to be the last hobbit on earth, rises to the challenge of wizard Gandalf to help recover a treasure stolen from his dwarf companions by the dragon Smaug. A complex, richly layered book that challenges children to track multiple characters and situations in a way that involves higher-level thinking skills. Hobbit devotees will go on to the trilogy Lord of the Rings: *The Fellowship of the Ring; The Two Towers;* and *The Return of the King.* **ADVANCED READERS.**

From the awards lists: look for Newbery award winners A Wrinkle in Time *by Madeline L'Engle (advanced readers) and* The Twenty-One Balloons *by William Pène du Bois.*

Growing Up Themes

Alcott, Louisa May. *Little Women*. The romantic classic about the four teen-aged March sisters—Meg, Jo, Beth, and Amy—who are waiting at home with their mother, Marmee, for their father to return from the battlefields of the Civil War. Most girls seem to fiercely identify with Jo, the tomboy writer who heads the family in their father's absence, and finds herself in all kinds of often amusing scrapes, many of which stem from the narrow societal roles of women at the time. This book will in all likelihood appear on a school reading list at some point, but it belongs on every bookshelf. Other lesser known Alcott "period pieces" introduce new families of characters with colorful stories as well, including *An Old-Fashioned Girl* and *Eight Cousins*.

Burnett, Frances Hodgson. *The Secret Garden*. Spoiled, sickly Mary Lennox is orphaned, yanked from her lonely but privileged upbringing in India, and sent to live with her reclusive uncle at forbidding Misselthwaite Manor. But through fresh air and exercise, a mystery hidden in a secret garden, and two new friends, Mary's healing begins and is eventually complete. Mary even becomes the catalyst for the healing of those around her. With its balance of male and female characters, this book appeals to both boys and girls. Burnett's second most popular novel, *A Little Princess*, will become dear to the hearts of girls primarily (if not just by virtue of the title, which, unfortunately, puts off some boys).

Cleaver, Vera and Bill. *Where the Lilies Bloom*. Illustrated by Jim Spanfeller. Under the leadership of fourteen-year-old Mary Call, the Luther family struggles to stay together in Depression-era Appalachia. Life seems tough enough without the additional challenge of having to conceal the death of their father from busybody neighbors who'd rather see Mary Call, Romey, Ima Dean, and Devola sent to live at the county home. This solid middle-grade novel about courage and family is often—and should be—required reading. Not only for its haunting story, but because it will stick with the reader for life.

Danziger, Paula. *Amber Brown Is Not a Crayon*. Illustrated by Tony Ross. Plucky third-grader Amber Brown gets teased about her crayon-color name, but having a best friend like Justin Daniels makes everything okay. Until the friends learn Justin's family is moving away. This contemporary book is a favorite with early-grade readers because it readably lays out the minefield that is elementary school with authenticity and humor. Amber handles her share of typical problems with a healthy sense of self, as evidenced in her retort to the childish name-calling: "Amber Brown is not a crayon. Amber Brown is a person." **EARLY GRADES. SERIES.**

Paterson, Katherine. *Come Sing, Jimmy Jo*. A middle-grade coming of age book that manages to be gritty and sweet at the same time. Eleven-year-old James—who later takes the stage name Jimmy Jo—lives with his adoring grandmother, but yearns to be a member of his family's country-western singing act. When he is discovered to have a golden voice, it lands him just that chance— but even his girlish mother envies his place in the limelight. Jimmy Jo sorts through his personal problems, which also come to include his grandmother's illness and his celebrity status at school, and emerges with admirable grace and maturity. You'll also want to check out Paterson's Newbery award winners *Bridge to Terabithia* and *Jacob Have I Loved*.

Stolz, Mary. *The Noonday Friends*. Illustrated by Louis S. Glanzman. Franny Davis longs to have a few nice things to wear, and to take her lunch to school instead of having to use a free lunch ticket. It would help too if she had more free time to spend with her best friend Simone Orgella—but her little brother Marshall needs her to look after him, and Franny's twin brother Jim is no help. The biggest problem all the Marshalls face is dreamy, artistic Mr. Marshall's inability to hold a job, and the demoralizing atmosphere his failures cast on the family. This readable and surprisingly bright novel gives an eagle-eye look into the life of a family whose riches are confined to seemingly endless reserves of hope. This story about loving people who have little is refreshing, and even important in the perspective it offers.

Streatfeild, Noel. *Ballet Shoes*. Illustrated by Richard Floethe, later by Diane Goode. Three unrelated female orphans are given the common surname Fossil and raised as sisters in the world of the theater. Pauline is a born actress, Posy a gifted dancer, and tomboyish Petrova is neither, but has instead an unbridled enthusiasm for cars and planes. Girls interested in performing arts of any kind, or who even just take dance lessons, will be enthralled by this easy-to-read, enduring book, and its vivid characters and exciting situations on and off stage. Other Streatfeild books about different characters include *Movie Shoes, Dancing Shoes,* and *Theatre Shoes*. **SERIES.**

Wilder, Laura Ingalls. *Little House in the Big Woods.* Illustrated by Garth Williams. Adults looking back on the most cherished books of their childhoods often remember this series with particular fondness. And, for parents seeking warm, well-written books that embrace simple "traditional family values" for their own children, Wilder delivers. The ten Little House books—which include *Little House on the Prairie, On the Banks of Plum Creek,* and *These Happy Golden Years*—are autobiographical in nature, and offer accurate descriptions of the isolated and often dangerous frontier life while chronicling the years of a loving pioneer family. And it's not too sappy. These books serve as strong, lively history lessons about what America really means. The virtues of hard work, family, and shared struggle can apply to any generation and culture in this country. By learning some about real world history, children can also learn something about themselves. **EARLY TO MIDDLE GRADES. SERIES.**

From the awards lists: look for Newbery award winners The Midwife's Apprentice *by Karen Cushman (early grades);* Bridge to Terabithia *by Katherine Paterson;* Roll of Thunder, Hear My Cry *by Mildred D. Taylor (which also has a "prequel" entitled* The Well: David's Story*); and* Up A Road Slowly *by Irene Hunt.*

Adventure

Alexander, Lloyd. *The Jedera Adventure.* In Vesper Holly's hands is evidence of a grave library offense—a book fifteen years overdue (never mind that it was her father, not one for small details, who checked it out). But the seemingly innocuous business of finally returning the book gives way to exciting adventure en route to the library in the North African country of Jedera. Vesper and her guardian Brinnie must deal with pesky problems like a biting camel and warring desert tribes on the way, but waiting for them in Jedera is a much larger challenge: that posed by evil Dr. Helvitius, who is plotting to tyrannize the world with a destructive invention. The prolific Alexander is renowned and beloved by young readers and educators alike for inventive, action-filled books and fine writing. Fans of Alexander's work should also look for his five-book Prydain Chronicles series (see description under Fantasy).

Christopher, John. *The White Mountains*. The first of a science fiction trilogy—next come *The City of Gold & Lead* and *The Pool of Fire*. A boy, his cousin, and a newfound friend band together to escape the evil Tripods from outer space in a futuristic tale about a quest for free will and personal choice. The author makes interesting use of the premise that though the formerly known civilization is gone—for instance, characters stumble on ancient underground networks the reader will recognize as subways—the various languages of the world stay intact. Aside from the exciting and involving story, the main characters' risking their lives to escape pervasive mind control techniques gives children a strong lesson to consider.

DeJong, Meindert. *The House of Sixty Fathers*. Illustrated by Maurice Sendak. The setting is China during the Japanese occupation years of World War II. Young Tien-Pao is alone on his family's boat when it pulls loose from its moorings and escapes into the rushing river. But when the boat settles, Tien-Pao finds himself in Japanese territory, with only his pet pig Glory-of-the-Republic for companionship. Together they must find Tien-Pao's lost family, while eluding Japanese troops. While getting lost in the breath-taking action and adventure of this novel, readers also will receive a fascinating history lesson.

Farmer, Nancy. *A Girl Named Disaster*. Eleven-year-old Nhamo faces a cruel fate for a girl of her tender age in here African society—she is about to be married to a mean man who already has other wives. So Nhamo flees to Zimbabwe. And as her grandmother predicts, the trip is not kind—Nhamo struggles to escape drowning, battles against possible starvation, and is almost overcome with loneliness. But in African tradition, the spirits and her dead mother comfort and guide her. A complex story of a coming-of-age experience that is both challenging and terrifying, the book also serves as an introduction to African folklore and culture. Featured at the back are a glossary of African terms; concise histories of the peoples of Zimbabwe and Mozambique; and a summary of the belief system of the Shona culture profiled in the book.

George, Jean Craighead. *My Side of the Mountain.* Illustrated by the author. Young Sam Gribley comes of age in near-solitude after running away from his New York home to the remote Catskill Mountains. In elegant though rustic style, he learns to live off the land his family once owned. And though it started out as just a daring experiment, young Sam emerges a true naturalist and survivor. This fine and famous book is frequently cited as a good family read-aloud and discussion choice.

Green, Roger Lancelyn. *The Adventures of Robin Hood.* For adventure purists, this is the classic 1956 retelling of the exciting and romantic legend of the outlaw who "stole from the rich and gave to the poor" in twelfth century England. Excerpts from old ballads preface each chapter and highlight the text, adding atmosphere and authenticity. **ADVANCED READERS.**

Paulsen, Gary. *Hatchet.* A realistic, beautifully told survival story of a thirteen-year-old boy stranded alone in the Canadian wilderness after a plane crash. To get by, Brian must rely on his one immediate possession: a hatchet. As he fights to stay alive, Brian also copes with his parents' divorce, his main preoccupation before his frightening personal adventure began.

Taylor, Theodore. *The Cay.* Phillip Enright, a twelve-year-old refugee from a ship torpedoed by a German submarine during World War II, is forced to take up a crude residence on a small Caribbean Island. The only other person around is Timothy, a grizzled, dignified West Indian native with a lilting calypso dialect. Phillip's challenging personal journey begins here. Not only has he absorbed his family's prejudice against dark-skinned people, but he finds himself utterly dependent on Timothy's care when he is suddenly blinded. This deeply moving story serves as a mini-course on survival and island ways and beliefs, as well as interracial tolerance.

From the awards lists: look for Newbery award winners The Whipping Boy *by Sid Fleischman (early grades) and* Island of the Blue Dolphins *by Scott O'Dell.*

Animals

Byars, Betsy. *The Midnight Fox.* Illustrated by Ann Grifalconi. When Tom's parents embark on a trip to Europe, the boy must stay on his aunt's and uncle's farm for the summer. First, he hates the prospect, and the reality seems even worse, with his Aunt Millie's expecting him to be an outdoor boy like her own sons, and his cousin Hazeline's annoying ways. But one day during a walk in the woods, Tom spots a beautiful black fox. Suddenly he is intrigued, and even manages to trace her back to her den and cub. So when the fox steals a turkey from the farm, and his uncle pledges to destroy the predator, Tom is moved to fiercely protect his wild animal friend. Byars powerfully illustrates the strong and real bonds that can form between humans and animals.

DeJong, Meindert. *Hurry Home, Candy.* Illustrated by Maurice Sendak. Elegantly written and highly readable story told from the point of view of a nameless stray dog that was once loved but has been separated from his family. This swiftly moving and compassionate book about the dog and the people he encounters—and his eventual rediscovery of security and trust—is often a read-aloud staple in living rooms and classrooms.

Farley, Walter. *The Black Stallion.* Illustrated by Keith Ward. When his ship docks at an Arabian port on the Red Sea, young Alec Ramsay spots a wild horse that will become his passion and accompany him on many exciting and dangerous adventures.
Note: The Black has been called "the most famous fictional

horse of the century." Farley began this book, the first of many, while a high school student in Brooklyn. He finished it and had it published before he was graduated from Columbia University. **SERIES.**

Grahame, Kenneth. *The Wind in the Willows.* Pastoral pals Toad, Mole, Water Rat and Badger cavort in the Wild Wood. Your child is sure to see people he knows in these wonderful characters—the petulant, unrepentant Toad; the faithful home-body Mole; and the sometimes wise and knowing Water Rat.

Henry, Marguerite. *Misty of Chincoteague.* Illustrated by Wesley Dennis. Based on real people, horses, and high adventure on two small islands off the coast of Virginia, this 1947 book has remained a literary treasure through more than thirty printings. In the beginning, ponies corralled in a Spanish galleon escape after a storm at sea, then swim ashore and roam wild on nearby Assateague Island. Youngsters Paul and Maureen Beebe are en-tranced by the wild horses, and one day Paul makes up his mind to capture one. **SERIES.**

North, Sterling. *Rascal.* The author's warm-hearted memoir about how, as an eleven-year-old boy, he spent a delightful year nurturing and being best buddies with a clever, mischievous baby raccoon. This is a remarkable story of friendship and letting go. For nature-lovers young and old.

Rawls, Wilson. *Where the Red Fern Grows.* For two years, Ozarks boy Billy Colman has carefully saved his money so he can buy two coon hounds. With time, he nurtures them into a fine hunting team known throughout his county, and eventually takes them to a hunting championship. But the success story turns tragic, and Billy learns a hard lesson about loss—and how a little bit of good can be found through the pain, as well as the bittersweet gift of memory. It probably doesn't need to be noted that this book is a tearjerker. Alas, animal stories so often are! But this is a beautifully told, mature book about the realities of life. **ADVANCED READERS.**

Note: Readers who enjoy this book should also look for Rawls' *Summer of the Monkeys*.

White, E.B. *Charlotte's Web*. Illustrated by Garth Williams. Childhood would not be complete without spending some time with Wilbur the pig and the magical spider Charlotte. This book is among the most well-written of books anywhere, with beautiful language and a sweet story perfect for either reading solo or aloud—preferably curled up at bedtime. Loyalty, devotion, and the value of sacrifice for others are lessons children see played out. The story begins as farm girl Fern saves the runt piglet of the litter from an early demise and names him Wilbur. But Wilbur's runt status is short lived and the growing pig ends up at the barnyard of a relative, where he makes many new friends led by a lovely gray spider named Charlotte.

Note: As a silent-reading follow-up, parents might recommend E.B. White's *The Trumpet of the Swan*, the story of an eleven-year-old naturalist whose life changes when he discovers a nest of trumpeter swans—and newborn cygnet Louis, who has no voice.

From the awards lists: look for Newbery award winners Shiloh *by Phyllis Reynolds Naylor and* Julie of the Wolves *by Jean Craighead George.*

Mystery/Scary

Bellairs, John. *The House With a Clock in Its Walls*. Illustrated by Edward Gorey. Ghosts, without the gore. Here is a superior, well-written Early Gothic substitute for children hooked on cheap horror. The reading level is higher than most of the horror series books. You might try reading the first few chapters aloud as a kick-off. Newly orphaned ten-year-old Lewis Barnavelt goes to live with his eccentric uncle Jonathan, a kindly magician who lives in an unusual old mansion. The two, along with Uncle Jonathan's magical friend Mrs. Zimmerman, solve the frightening mystery of a clock that has been embedded in the mansion walls by a sinister warlock. Two other books complete a trilogy:

The Figure in the Shadows, and *The Letter, the Witch, and the Ring*. Though written in novel style with rich characterization and lots of humor, these books have eerie edges. Look for other Lewis Barnavelt books, as well as many other Bellairs works including *The Drum, the Doll and the Zombie*, and *The Ghost in the Mirror*. **SERIES.**

Erwin, Betty K. *Who Is Victoria?* Illustrated by Kathleen Anderson. Margaret and her friends try to find out the secret of Victoria, a lively, old-fashioned girl who seems to have appeared from nowhere. Though currently out of print, this book can easily be found in libraries and makes this list because of the memorable and satisfying story, by turns eerie and hilarious. At the end, the reader is surprised and pleased by a revelation about an old woman's fervent desire to be young again.

Fleischman, Sid. *The Ghost on Saturday Night*. Illustrated by Laura Cornell. When the slick Professor Pepper gives Opie tickets to the ghost-raising of Crookneck John in return for leading him out of a thick fog, Opie and his Aunt Etta take up the invitation. But when the famous outlaw's ghost escapes, the terrified audience quickly scatters, and Opie is left to help thwart a would-be clever bank robbery. This chapter book, and other similarly harmless "scary" Fleischman stories—like *The Midnight Horse*, *The Ghost in the Noonday Sun,* and *The 13th Floor: A Ghost Story*—make lively, wonderfully written reads for early- to middle-graders. **EARLY TO MIDDLE GRADES.**
Note: Fleischman, also author of the Newbery award winning *The Whipping Boy*, wrote the delightful McBroom tall tale series you may remember seeing lining the shelves during your own childhood. His son is Paul Fleischman, who also won a Newbery award, for *Joyful Noise: Poems for Two Voices*.

Howe, Deborah and James. *Bunnicula: A Rabbit Tale of Mystery*. Illustrated by Alan Daniel. Clever, funny modern classic about how an intellectual family with two boys finds a bunny in a movie theater—and how it changes the household forever, perhaps not for the better. To the other house pets, a slightly paranoid cat with an overactive imagination, and a long-suffering dog who previously enjoyed his status as the responsible fixture of the family, the bunny is quite threatening indeed. For one, he's sucking up all the attention. Second, he's of questionable origin—the note attached to the box he was left in reveals he was from Transylvania. *Bunnicula* has sequels, *The Celery Stalks at Midnight* and *Howliday Inn*. **EARLY TO MIDDLE GRADES.**

Konigsburg, E. L. *Jennifer, Hecate, Macbeth, William McKinley, and Me, Elizabeth*. Illustrated by the author. A lonely only child, Elizabeth, is delighted to befriend Jennifer, a sophisticated, aloof girl who claims to be a witch. But when Elizabeth embarks on her make-believe witch's apprenticeship, many sticky situations ensue. And even her friendship with Jennifer is threatened. Under the funny overlay of adventure runs a primary theme about the nature and importance of friendship and the need to belong.

Peck, Richard. *The Ghost Belonged to Me*. Thirteen-year-old Alexander, a wealthy boy living in the turn-of-the-century Midwest, is both blessed and plagued with his gift of second sight. But when a spooky mystery crops up involving the ghost of a southern belle, he must reluctantly accept assistance from fellow seer Blossom Culp, who along with other liabilities, is sweet on Alexander. Like the characters in the best children's books, the intelligent and street savvy Blossom—who is the worthy main character in several other of Peck's books—is the embodiment of good-humored self-reliance. She shows that a girl need not have a privileged upbringing—nor even be liked by the boy of her choice—to have an exciting life. Look for other books starring Blossom and Alexander, including *Ghosts I Have Been*—which features a spooky side-story about the Titanic—and *The Dreadful Future of Blossom Culp*. **SERIES.**

Snyder, Zilpha Keatley. *The Headless Cupid*. Illustrated by Alton Raible. The four young Stanleys, children of a financially struggling professor, get more than they bargain for when they meet their new stepsister Amanda. When haughty Amanda arrives at their rambling, ramshackle house in ceremonial costume complete with a crow she refers to as her Familiar, and then announces she is a serious student of the occult, the Stanleys decide the only way to figure out their new stepsister might just be to join her for a while. The sticky situations that ensue during their make-believe apprenticeships are laugh-out-loud funny. But things really turn eerie when they stumble on a mystery about the cupid statue on the stairway. Another book about the Stanley family is *The Famous Stanley Kidnapping Case*. Also look for Snyder's many books starring different characters, such as her critically acclaimed novel *The Egypt Game*. **SERIES.**

Sobol, Donald J. Encyclopedia Brown solve-it-yourself mystery stories. Various illustrators. With titles like *Encyclopedia Brown Gets His Man*, and *Encyclopedia Brown and the Case of Pablo's Nose*, these engaging and challenging solve-it-yourselfers provide young mystery lovers hours and hours of using their heads—without even realizing it! Each book starring Leroy "Encyclopedia" Brown, the son of the town police chief, contains a number of brief mystery scenarios, whose solutions can be found at the back of the book. **EARLY TO MIDDLE GRADES.**

From the awards lists: look for Coretta Scott King award winner The Dark-Thirty: Southern Tales of the Supernatural *by Patricia McKissack and Newbery Award winner* The Westing Game *by Ellen Raskin.*

(Also be sure to see our section Fresh Alternatives in the chapter Luring the Reluctant Reader and The Junk Book Junkie for other scary book suggestions, p. 43.)

Everyday Kids

Cleary, Beverly. *Ramona the Pest*. Illustrated by Louis Darling. Children typically opt for stories about kids older than themselves, but the hilarious, hair-raising tales about five-year-old Ramona Quimby—and the headaches she causes everyone around her, especially her big sister Beezus—are an exception. When

Ramona's new kindergarten teacher tells her to "sit here for the present," Ramona waits for a gift; and when Ramona finds a pink worm on the playground, she wraps it around her finger and dubs it an "engagement ring." Look for other Ramona books including *Beezus and Ramona* and *Ramona the Brave*. Early-grade readers will quickly seek other books in the series about the children of Klickitat Street (see note below). **EARLY GRADES. SERIES.**

Note: Ramona fans, and boy readers, will want to check out Cleary's Henry books, starting with *Henry Huggins*. In it, third-grader Henry finds a skinny stray dog he names Ribsy, who changes his life forever. This book's endearing characters and crackling humor are in keeping with that shown in the Ramona books; yet boys in particular will relate to this male main character.

Enright, Elizabeth. *The Four Story Mistake.* The four Melendy children suffer culture shock when their father moves them from a comfortable brownstone in New York City to a curious "four story mistake" of a house in the country. But once the children come to terms with the new environment, they discover rural living and the opportunities it offers can be interesting and even exciting. Other popular books about the Melendys are *The Saturdays* and *Then There Were Five*.

Estes, Eleanor. *The Hundred Dresses.* Illustrated by Louis Slobodkin. When new classmate Wanda Petronski, with her funny name and single faded dress, claims to have one hundred other dresses at home all lined up in her closet, everyone snickers and thinks she's lying. But Wanda's story—and her integrity—are revealed in a startlingly creative way. This absorbing and sensitively written book about the nature of children and ethnic prejudice has a message so clear as to seem a bit preachy to adults. But the lesson about the differences among people is valuable and easily digested by children. **EARLY GRADES.**

Note: Also look for prolific Estes' other books, such as *The Moffats*, *The Middle Moffat*, *Rufus M.,* and *Pinky Pye*, and the Newbery award-winning *Ginger Pye*.

Fitzhugh, Louise. *Harriet the Spy*. In her quest to become a famous writer when she grows up, sixth-grader Harriet keeps a secret notebook of "observations" about her classmates and family. But her life descends into turmoil when her beloved nursemaid Ole Golly leaves, and her classmates find her journal—and in it, the less-than-glowing remarks Harriet has recorded about them. A dead-on, elegantly written book that gives legitimacy to the aspirations and problems of children. Though written in the 1960s, this book has a modern feel, as evidenced by a recent movie adaptation.

Haywood, Carolyn. *B Is for Betsy*. Illustrated by the author. Many of these circa 1940s and 50s books remain in print, with updated covers. Others can easily be found in most libraries. Wholesome and readable, with involving and often humorous stories about real (and very good, for the most part) children, these are the kinds of books that get read over and over again and become fondly remembered in adulthood. Though these books are dated in many ways, the characters hold true and their escapades still enchant and engross early grade readers. That's why they're still on the bookstore shelves. Other Betsy books include *Back to School With Betsy* and *Betsy and the Boys*. **EARLY GRADES. SERIES.**

Note: Boys who more readily take to male protagonists might enjoy Haywood's series featuring Eddie, including *Ever-Ready Eddie* and *Eddie's Green Thumb*. They should easily be found in the library.

Lord, Bette Bao. *In the Year of the Boar and Jackie Robinson*. Illustrated by Marc Simont. Though born in China, Shirley Temple Wong must adjust to post World War II American life after her father gets a job in Brooklyn. But alas, the American ways differ from the more stiff and ceremonious Chinese ones. Readers will laugh out loud at Shirley's recitation of the Pledge of Allegiance ("I pledge a lesson to the frog …") This touching, humor-filled book about cultural differences lets readers gently laugh at Shirley's efforts, while drawing empathy for her tough situation— and applause for the progress she makes. Young baseball fans also will cheer Shirley's acquired devotion to the Brooklyn Dodgers, which ultimately serves as the cultural equalizer in this story.

Lovelace, Maud Hart. *Betsy-Tacy*. Illustrated by Lois Lenski. The ever-popular Betsy-Tacy books follow the best-friend characters from childhood through high school and even into marriage, which makes for long-term appeal and fond memories for generations of girls. The first is a chapter book, but the books graduate into more advanced reading as the characters age. Other titles include *Betsy-Tacy and Tib*, *Heaven to Betsy*, and *Betsy's Wedding*. **EARLY TO MIDDLE GRADES. SERIES.**

Taylor, Sydney. *All-of-a-Kind Family*. Illustrated by Helen John. Charming and absorbing day-to-day activities of a large Jewish family of five girls ages four to twelve living on New York's Lower East Side. Girls especially will enjoy following this interesting family through sequels including *All-of-a-Kind Family Downtown*, and *All-of-a-Kind Family Uptown*. Parents will appreciate the carefully and lovingly detailed view into World War I-era Jewish family life and customs, and the happy relationships these books depict. **SERIES.**

From the awards lists: look for Newbery award winners Dear Mr. Henshaw *by Beverly Cleary (early grades) and* From the Mixed-Up Files of Mrs. Basil E. Frankweiler *by E.L. Konigsburg.*

(For more alternatives to series books like Babysitters Club and Sweet Valley High, be sure to look for our alternative lists in the chapter Luring the Reluctant Reader and the Junk Book Junkie, p. 43.)

Non-Fiction Books

Ballard, Robert D. *Exploring the Titanic*. This book describes the "unsinkable" luxury liner that sank on its maiden voyage in 1912, and the discovery and exploration of its underwater wreckage. The man who actually located and first dived to the wreck, Ballard has always had deep respect for the bones and lost possessions of the ships whose locations he has sought. The explorer has refused to disturb their watery graves (although, as we all know, the sites have been plundered by later visitors, a fact known to disturb Ballard and other Titanic historians).

Cole, Joanna. The Magic School Bus science series. Illustrated by Bruce Degen. In titles such as *The Magic School Bus: Inside the Human Body*, and *The Magic School Bus: Lost in the Solar System*, eccentric but exceptionally well-informed teacher Miss Frizzle whisks students both reluctant and gung-ho on a new science-related adventure at every opportunity. The richly detailed illustrations are a real treat—note how Miss Frizzle's shoes and outfits match each new adventure. Children can spend many minutes ferreting out the little jokes within the margins of the illustrations. Further, some children have a natural interest in science—but these books boil down scientific concepts to plain terms every child can understand and enjoy. **SERIES.**

Fritz, Jean. *Shh! We're Writing the Constitution*. Illustrated by Tomie dePaola. A detailed and fascinating—and highly readable—chronicle of how the original thirteen "sovereign states" managed to agree to become a nation. All the characters are here, from George Washington to Benjamin Franklin to Patrick Henry, and with them colorful anecdotes and pictures. Adults will appreciate this history lesson, too. Look for other history books by Fritz, including *What's the Big Idea, Ben Franklin?*, and *Will You Sign Here, John Hancock?* **EARLY TO MIDDLE GRADES.**

Greenfeld, Howard. *Books: From Writer to Reader*. An introduction to the complicated and intriguing business of bookmaking, from the writing to production and printing, to the bookstore and the hands of the reader. This classic book also examines how designers choose typefaces, how pages are composed, even how color is printed and how the pages are glued together. There's also a section on desktop publishing. Publishing technology and the business itself changes quickly, so some steps will seem dated, but most of the material holds true. **MIDDLE-GRADE TO ADVANCED READERS.**

Peet, Bill. *Bill Peet: An Autobiography*. All about prolific and popular picture book author Bill Peet (see *The Whingdingdilly* in the picture book section). Peet spent a large chunk of his adult life as one of the top sketch and story artists for Walt Disney's most famous animated features, including *Cinderella, Dumbo,* and *Pinocchio*. In this book, Peet uses his art—in true storyboard style—as much as his words to describe his life, from a carefree childhood to a lonely adolescence, to his exciting and often frustrating years as a brilliant and under-recognized artist, and finally to international success as a juvenile author. He includes the people he met along the way, such as his wife Margaret and, of course, Walt Disney. This makes a grand first biography for children to read, far preferable to the often lackluster series about famous historical figures. The book is approachable because of the energetic drawings and clear, simple language.

Schwartz, David M. *If You Made a Million*. Illustrated by Steven Kellogg. This practical picture book for financial-wizards-to-be (or children who could profit from an early lesson in basic finance) describes money in its various forms, from coins to paper to checks. Marvelissimo the Mathematical Magician goes on to show how money enables purchases, pays off loans or builds interest at the bank. A great book for when it comes time to negotiate that first allowance or a child-financed trip to the store. **EARLY GRADES.**

Sis, Peter. *Starry Messenger: A Book Depicting the Life of a Famous Scientist, Mathematician, Astronomer, Philosopher, Physicist, Galileo Galilei*. Beautifully crafted and illustrated picture book about the life and work of Galileo. This book can be read on two levels. The main text tells Galileo's story in very approachable style, while the notes from his writings and facts about his life incorporated in the lovely pictures go deeper for older children and adults.

From the awards lists: look for Coretta Scott King award winner Long Hard Journey: The Story of the Pullman Porter *by Patricia and Fredrick McKissack, and Newbery Award winners* Invincible Louisa: The Story of the Author of Little Women *by Cornelia Meigs.*

Note: *The Coretta Scott King awards list includes many nonfiction works about African-American heritage, including biographies and autobiographies of famous African-Americans including The Reverend Martin Luther King Jr., singer Ray Charles, baseball great Jackie Robinson, and poet Langston Hughes.*

Books of Poetry

Selected by de Regniers, Beatrice Schenk, Eva Moore, Mary Michaels White, and Jan Carr. *Sing a Song of Popcorn: Every Child's Book of Poems.* Illustrated by nine Caldecott Medal artists including Maurice Sendak, Arnold Lobel, and Marc Simont. Gorgeously illustrated and imaginatively organized anthology that introduces more than one hundred poems ranging from ancient to contemporary in themes: from animals to nonsense to spooky to extremely brief. Poets include Eve Mirriam, Edna St. Vincent Millay, and Robert Louis Stevenson.

Joseph, Lynn. *Coconut Kind of Day: Island Poems.* Illustrated by Sandra Speidel. A must-have for any early collector of poetry. This excellent and explosively colorful picture book of short poems about the daily experiences of a young girl in Trinidad makes the sights, sounds and tastes of Caribbean culture come alive. Parents and children alike will find themselves returning to this collection over and over for quick island getaways, and even babies enjoy the rhythms and colors.

Kennedy, X.J., and Dorothy M. Kennedy. *Knock at a Star: A Child's Introduction to Poetry*. Illustrated by Karen Ann Weinhaus. Poetry can make a child laugh, make him wonder, or tell a story … . This approachable book offers a superb selection of child-friendly but challenging poetry including poems by William Carlos Williams, Gwendolyn Brooks, and Ogden Nash. But this book also shows children exactly how poetry accomplishes what it does, in a straightforward, non-didactic way. To begin cultivating appreciation for poetry in you and your child, this book is a great place to start.

Prelutsky, Jack. *The New Kid on the Block*. Illustrated by James Stevenson. From "Jellyfish Stew" to "Song of the Gloopy Gloppers" to "Ballad of a Boneless Chicken," these rollicking, off-the-wall rhymes and amusing drawings will tickle everyone from reader to listener. These poems are as kid-friendly and approachable (à la Shel Silverstein) as any you'll find.
Note: Also look for Prelutsky's *The Dragons Are Singing Tonight*, illustrated by Peter Sis.

Silverstein, Shel. *Where the Sidewalk Ends*. This is an extremely popular collection by Silverstein where one can read about washing one's shadow, or planting a diamond garden, or putting up one's sister for sale, and meet new characters like Hector the Collector and Ridiculous Rose. This is a book to savor in small, delicious bites, read aloud by an older reader or by the children to themselves. Also look for Silverstein's *A Light in the Attic*.

From the awards lists: look for Coretta Scott King award winner Soul Looks Back in Wonder, *a compilation of Afrocentric poetry collected and illustrated by Tom Feelings; and Newbery award winners* Joyful Noise: Poems For Two Voices *by Paul Fleischman, illustrated by Eric Beddows, and* A Visit to William Blake's Inn: Poems for Innocent and Experienced Travelers *by Nancy Willard.*

Award Winning Books

NOTE: Though a Newbery, Caldecott, Coretta Scott King, or state book award is a good—not to mention prestigious—indicator of a well-written children's book, a comparison with the books on our master list will show that the books that are not major award-winners are often just as good, or even better. Prolific children's author Jane Yolen has referred to the Caldecott medal her book *Owl Moon* won as "fairy dust." Though *Owl Moon* has almost reached modern classic status, her implication is that many books are worthy; a few get lucky.

So although award winners make a fine starting point, we urge you to look and think beyond the medals. Certainly, any book that has won a big quality award probably can be presumed to be well-written literature. But as they say, some are more equal than others. Go back and forth. You'll see the master list includes cross-references to recommended award books that fall under the categories we've made. Also, Newbery Honor and Caldecott Honor books (the runners-up) are often terrific. Many on our list have been runners-up.

Following are brief descriptions of this country's major children's book awards:

Caldecott Medal

Established in 1938 and named after Nineteenth-century English illustrator Randolph Caldecott, the Caldecott Medal is presented annually for the most distinguished children's picture book published in America the previous year. The prize is awarded for illustrations, though text and story are often taken into account. The award is administered by the Association for Library Service to Children, a division of the American Library Association.

Newbery Medal

The Newbery Medal is named for John Newbery, an Eighteenth-century English bookseller, and is awarded annually by the American Library Association for the most distinguished American children's book (usually a novel, but sometimes a work of nonfiction or a poetry collection) published the previous year. Introduced in 1922, the Newbery medal was the first children's book award in the world and continues to be the most recognized and talked about in America.

Coretta Scott King awards

Established in 1969, the Coretta Scott King Book Awards are presented annually to one African-American author and one African-American illustrator. Historically, most awards have recognized juvenile work, both fiction and nonfiction; some have singled out young adult books; and a few have been given for adult books. The awards program was founded to honor Coretta Scott King's ongoing work to promote world peace, as well as to commemorate the life and work of Dr. Martin Luther King Jr. The program further seeks to promote appreciation and understanding of the societal and creative contributions and culture of African-American people. The book awards are administered by the Social Responsibilities Round Table of the American Library Association.

Caldecott Medal Winners
1938-1998

1998   *Rapunzel*, Paul O. Zelinsky

1997   *Golem*, David Wisniewski

1996   *Officer Buckle and Gloria*, Peggy Rathman

1995   *Smoky Night*, Eve Bunting, illustrated by David Diaz

1994   *Grandfather's Journey*, Allen Say

1993   *Mirette on the High Wire*, Emily Arnold McCully

1992   *Tuesday*, David Wiesner

1991   *Black and White*, David Macaulay

1990   *Lon Po Po: A Red-Riding Hood Story from China*, Ed Young

1989   *Song & Dance Man*, Karen Ackerman, illustrated by Stephen Gammell

1988   *Owl Moon*, Jane Yolen, illustrated by John Schoenherr

1987   *Hey, Al*, Arthur Yorinks, illustrated by Richard Egielski

1986   *The Polar Express*, Chris Van Allsburg

1985   *Saint George and the Dragon*, Margaret Hodges, illustrated by Trina Schart Hyman

1984   *The Glorious Flight: Across the Channel with Louis Blériot*, Alice & Martin Provensen

1983   *Shadow*, Blaise Cendrars, illustrated by Marcia Brown

1982   *Jumanji*, Chris Van Allsburg

1981   *Fables*, Arnold Lobel

1980   *The Ox-Cart Man,* Donald Hall, illustrated by Barbara Cooney

1979   *The Girl Who Loved Wild Horses*, Paul Goble

1978   *Noah's Ark*, Jacob Revius, illustrated by Peter Spirer

1977   *Ashanti to Zulu: African Traditions*, Margaret Musgrove, illustrated by Leo and Diane Dillon

1976   *Why Mosquitoes Buzz in People's Ears: A West African Tale*, Verna Aardema, illustrated by Leo and Diane Dillon

1975   *Arrow to the Sun: A Pueblo Indian Tale*, Gerald McDermott

1974   *Duffy and the Devil*, Harve Zemach, illustrated by Margot Zemach

1973 *The Funny Little Woman*, Arlene Mosel, illustrated by Blair Lent

1972 *One Fine Day*, Nonny Hogrogian

1971 *A Story—A Story*, Gail E. Haley

1970 *Sylvester and the Magic Pebble*, William Steig

1969 *The Fool of the World and the Flying Ship*, Arthur Ransome, illustrated by Uri Shulevitz

1968 *Drummer Hoff*, Barbara Emberley, illustrated by Ed Emberley

1967 *Sam, Bangs and Moonshine,* Evaline Ness

1966 *Always Room for One More*, Sorche Nic Leodhas, illustrated by Nonny Hogrogian

1965 *May I Bring A Friend?*, Beatrice Schenk de Regniers, illustrated by Beni Montresor

1964 *Where The Wild Things Are*, Maurice Sendak

1963 *The Snowy Day*, Ezra Jack Keats

1962 *Once A Mouse*, Marcia Brown

1961 *Baboushka and the Three Kings*, Ruth Robbins, illustrated by Nicolas Sidjakov

1960 *Nine Days to Christmas*, Marie Hall Ets and Aurora Labastida, illustrated by Marie Hall Ets

1959 *Chanticleer and the Fox,* adapted from Geoffrey Chaucer, illustrated by Barbara Cooney

1958 *Time of Wonder*, Robert McCloskey

1957 *A Tree is Nice*, Janice May Udry, illustrated by Marc Simont

1956 *Frog Went A-Courtin'*, John Langstaff, illustrated by Feodor Rojankovsky

1955 *Cinderella, or, The Little Glass Slipper*, Charles Perrault, illustrated by Marcia Brown

1954 *Madeline's Rescue*, Ludwig Bemelmans

1953 *The Biggest Bear*, Lynd K. Ward

1952 *Finders Keepers*, William Lipkind, illustrated by Nicolas Mordvinoff

1951 *The Egg Tree*, Katherine Milhous

1950 *Song of the Swallows*, Leo Politi

1949 *The Big Snow*, Berta and Elmer Hader

1948 *White Snow, Bright Snow*, Alvin Tresselt, illustrated by Roger Duvoisin

1947 *The Little Island*, Golden MacDonald (Margaret Wise Brown), illustrated by Leonard Weisgard
1946 *The Rooster Crows*, Maud and Miska Petersham
1945 *Prayer For A Child*, Rachel Field, illustrated by Elizabeth Orton Jones
1944 *Many Moons*, James Thurber, illustrated by Louis Slobodkin
1943 *The Little House*, Virginia Lee Burton
1942 *Make Way for Ducklings*, Robert McCloskey
1941 *They Were Strong and Good*, Robert Lawson
1940 *Abraham Lincoln*, Ingri and Edgar Parin d'Aulaire
1939 *Mei Li*, Thomas Handforth
1938 *Animals of the Bible*, Dorothy Lathrop

Newbery Medal Winners
1922—1998

1998 *Out of the Dust*, Karen Hesse
1997 *The View From Saturday*, E.L. Konigsburg
1996 *The Midwife's Apprentice*, Karen Cushman
1995 *Walk Two Moons*, Sharon Creech
1994 *The Giver*, Lois Lowry
1993 *Missing May*, Cynthia Rylant
1992 *Shiloh*, Phyllis Reynolds Naylor
1991 *Maniac Magee*, Jerry Spinelli
1990 *Number the Stars*, Lois Lowry
1989 *Joyful Noise: Poems for Two Voices*, Paul Fleischman
1988 *Lincoln: A Photobiography*, Russell Freedman
1987 *The Whipping Boy*, Sid Fleischman
1986 *Sarah, Plain and Tall*, Patricia MacLachlan
1985 *The Hero and the Crown*, Robin McKinley
1984 *Dear Mr. Henshaw*, Beverly Cleary
1983 *Dicey's Song*, Cynthia Voigt
1982 *A Vist to William Blake's Inn: Poems for Innocent and Experienced Travelers*, Nancy Willard
1981 *Jacob Have I Loved*, Katherine Paterson

1980 *A Gathering Of Days: A New England Girl's Journal, 1830-32*, Joan Blos

1979 *The Westing Game*, Ellen Raskin

1978 *Bridge to Terabithia*, Katherine Paterson

1977 *Roll of Thunder, Hear My Cry*, Mildred D. Taylor

1976 *The Grey King*, Susan Cooper

1975 *M.C. Higgins, the Great*, Virginia Hamilton

1974 *The Slave Dancer*, Paula Fox

1973 *Julie of the Wolves*, Jean Craighead George

1972 *Mrs. Frisby and the Rats of NIMH*, Robert C. O'Brien

1971 *The Summer Of The Swans*, Betsy Byars

1970 *Sounder*, William H. Armstrong

1969 *The High King*, Lloyd Alexander

1968 *From the Mixed-Up Files of Mrs. Basil E. Frankweiler*, E.L. Konigsburg

1967 *Up A Road Slowly*, Irene Hunt

1966 *I, Juan de Pareja*, Elizabeth Borton de Treviño

1965 *Shadow of a Bull,* Maia Wojciechowska

1964 *It's Like This, Cat*, Emily C. Neville

1963 *A Wrinkle in Time*, Madeline L'Engle

1962 *The Bronze Bow*, Elizabeth George Speare

1961 *Island of the Blue Dolphins*, Scott O'Dell

1960 *Onion John*, John Krumgold

1959 *The Witch of Blackbird Pond*, Elizabeth George Speare

1958 *Rifles for Watie*, Harold V. Keith

1957 *Miracles on Maple Hill*, Virginia Sorensen

1956 *Carry On, Mr. Bowditch*, Jean Lee Latham

1955 *The Wheel on the School*, Meindert DeJong

1954 *...And Now Miguel*, John Krumgold

1953 *Secret of the Andes*, Ann Nolan Clark

1952 *Ginger Pye*, Eleanor Estes

1951 *Amos Fortune, Free Man*, Elizabeth Yates

1950 *The Door in the Wall*, Marguerite de Angeli

1949 *King of the Wind*, Marguerite Henry

1948 *The Twenty-One Balloons*, William Pène du Bois

1947 *Miss Hickory*, Carolyn S. Bailey

1946 *Strawberry Girl*, Lois Lenski

1945 *Rabbit Hill*, Robert Lawson

1944 *Johnny Tremain*, Esther Forbes
1943 *Adam of the Road*, Elizabeth Janet Gray
1942 *The Matchlock Gun*, Walter D. Edmonds
1941 *Call it Courage*, Armstrong Sperry
1940 *Daniel Boone*, James Daugherty
1939 *Thimble Summer*, Elizabeth Enright
1938 *The White Stag*, Kate Seredy
1937 *Roller Skates*, Ruth Sawyer
1936 *Caddie Woodlawn*, Carol Ryrie Brink
1935 *Dobry*, Monica Shannon
1934 *Invincible Louisa: The Story of the Author of Little Women*, Cornelia Meigs
1933 *Young Fu of the Upper Yangtze*, Elizabeth Lewis
1932 *Waterless Mountain*, Laura Adams Armer
1931 *The Cat Who Went to Heaven*, Elizabeth Coatsworth
1930 *Hitty, Her First Hundred Years*, Rachel Field
1929 *The Trumpeter of Krakow: A Tale of the Fifteenth Century*, Eric P. Kelly
1928 *Gay-Neck, the Story of a Pigeon*, Dhan Mukerji
1927 *Smoky, the Cow Horse*, Will James
1926 *Shen of the Sea*, Arthur Chrisman
1925 *Tales From Silver Lands*, Charles Finger
1924 *The Dark Frigate*, Charles Hawes
1923 *The Voyages of Doctor Dolittle*, Hugh Lofting
1922 *The Story of Mankind*, Hendrik Van Loon

Coretta Scott King Book Awards
1970-1998

(In years or categories not listed, the award went for adult books, or none was given. Note: Prior to 1979, separate awards were not given for illustrations.)

1998 *Forged by Fire*, Sharon M. Draper; *In Daddy's Arms I Am Tall: African Americans Celebrating Fathers*, illustrated by

Javaka Steptoe [The latter is a series of poems about fatherhood. The former is a young adult novel.]

1997 *Slam!*, Walter Dean Myers; *Minty: A Story of Young Harriet Tubman*, Alan Schroeder, illustrated by Jerry Pinckney

1996 *Her Stories*, Virginia Hamilton, illustrated by Leo and Diane Dillon; *The Middle Passage: White Ships Black Cargo*, illustrated by Tom Feelings (introduction by John Henrik Clarke)

1995 *Christmas in the Big House, Christmas in the Quarters*, Patricia C. and Fredrick L. McKissack; *The Creation*, James Weldon Johnson, illustrated by James Ransome

1994 *Toning the Sweep*, Angela Johnson; *Soul Looks Back in Wonder*, Tom Feelings (for illustrations)

1993 *The Dark-Thirty: Southern Tales of the Supernatural*, Patricia McKissack; *The Origin of Life on Earth: An African Creation Myth*, David A. Anderson, illustrated by Kathleen Atkins Wilson

1992 *Now Is Your Time! The African-American Struggle for Freedom*, Walter Dean Myers; *Tar Beach*, Faith Ringgold (for illustrations)

1991 *The Road to Memphis*, Mildred D. Taylor; *Aida*, Leontyne Price, illustrated by Leo & Diane Dillon

1990 *A Long Hard Journey: The Story of the Pullman Porter*, Patricia and Fredrick McKissack; *Nathaniel Talking*, Eloise Greenfield, illustrated by Jan Spivey Gilchrist

1989 *Fallen Angels*, Walter Dean Myers; *Mirandy and Brother Wind*, Patricia McKissack, illustrated by Jerry Pinckney

1988 *The Friendship*, Mildred D. Taylor; *Mufaro's Beautiful Daughters: An African Tale*, John Steptoe (for illustrations)

1987 *Justin and the Best Biscuits in The World*, Mildred Pitts Walter; *Half a Moon and One Whole Star*, Crescent Dragonwagon, illustrated by Jerry Pinckney

1986 *The People Could Fly: American Black Folktales*, Virginia Hamilton; *The Patchwork Quilt*, Valerie Flournoy, illustrated by Jerry Pinckney

1985 *Motown and Didi*, Walter Dean Myers

1984   *Everett Anderson's Goodbye*, Lucille Clifton; *My Mama Needs Me*, Mildred Pitts Walter, illustrated by Pat Cummings

1983   *Sweet Whispers, Brother Rush*, Virginia Hamilton; *Black Child*, Peter Magubane (for illustrations)

1982   *Let the Circle Be Unbroken*, Mildred D. Taylor; *Mother Crocodile: An Uncle Amadou Tale From Senegal* adapted by Rosa Guy, illustrated by John Steptoe

1981   *This Life*, Sidney Poitier; *Beat the Story—Drum, Pum Pum*, Ashley Bryan (for illustrations)

1980   *The Young Landlords*, Walter Dean Myers; *Cornrows*, Camille Yarbrough, illustrated by Carole Byard

1979   *Escape to Freedom: A Play About Young Frederick Douglass*, Ossie Davis; *Something on My Mind*, Nikki Grimes, illustrated by Tom Feelings

1978   *Africa Dream*, Eloise Greenfield, illustrated by Carole Byard

1977   *The Story of Stevie Wonder*, James Haskins

1976   *Duey's Tale*, Pearl Bailey

1975   *The Legend of Africania*, Dorothy Robinson, illustrated by Herbert Temple

1974   *Ray Charles*, Sharon Bell Mathis, illustrated by George Ford

1973   *I Never Had It Made: The Autobiography of Jackie Robinson*, Jackie Robinson, as told to Alfred Duckett

1972   *Seventeen Black Artists*, Elton C. Fax

1971   *Black Troubador: Langston Hughes*, Charlemae H. Rollins

1970   *Martin Luther King, Jr.: Man of Peace*, Lillie Paterson

Recommended Children's Book and Reading Resources

CHILDREN'S BOOK CATALOGS

Chinaberry Book Service—Highly selective and personalized children's book catalog, with comprehensive book descriptions and helpful reading tips.
  2780 Via Orange Way
  Suite B
  Spring Valley, CA 91978
  1-800-776-2242

Cherry Valley Books—Internet-based children's bookstore and on-line catalog that offers handpicked children's and parenting books along with reviews and customer comments. An e-mail newsletter also is available.
  www.cherryvalleybooks.com
  1-888-793-9481

CHILDREN'S BOOK CLUB

Children's Book of the Month Club—A division of the larger Book of the Month Club, with the standard classics and children's favorites.
Customer Service Center
Camp Hill, PA 17012-0001
(To receive a brochure or catalog, send a note with your address and return information. Also, you'll often see their brochures in parenting magazines, newspaper ads, and direct mailings.)

AUDIOBOOK COMPANIES

Listening Library, Inc.—Offers extensive selection of unabridged recordings of Newbery Award-winning novels, as well as other highly acclaimed children's books, classics, and special "read-along" titles.
One Park Avenue
Old Greenwich, CT 06870-1727
www.listeninglib.com
1-800-243-4504

Recorded Books, Inc.—Comprehensive, well chosen audiobook collection of some of the finest children's books.
270 Skipjack Road
Prince Frederick, MD 20678
www.recordedbooks.com
1-800-638-1304

CHILDREN'S BOOK REVIEWS

For reviews of new books, consult these publications:

The Bulletin of the Center for Children's Books—Library periodical published monthly by the University of Illinois Graduate School of Library and Information Science. For information write:
University of Illinois Press
325 S. Oak
Champaign, IL 61820

The Horn Book Magazine—Library periodical published bi-monthly. For subscription information, write:

The Horn Book Inc.
Circulation Department
56 Roland St., Suite 200
Boston, MA 02129
1-800-325-1170

School Library Journal—Considered the industry standard. Reviews most books, as well as CD-ROMs and other computer software, and Internet sites. For subscription information, write:

PO Box 57559
Boulder, CO 80322-7554
1-800-456-9409

CHILDREN'S MAGAZINES

Cricket—Geared for ages nine-fourteen, this is one of the more literary children's magazines, featuring short stories, poetry, nonfiction pieces, and reader recommendations of favorite books. Offshoots include *Babybug* (for ages six months—two years); *Ladybug* (ages two-six); and *Spider* (ages six-nine).

PO Box 7433
Red Oak, IA 51591
www.cricketmag.com
1-800-827-0227

Highlights for Children—Well-rounded monthly children's magazine geared to a broad age group and designed to flex thinking skills with nonfiction pieces and stories, riddles, jokes, and games. For new subscription information write:

PO Box 269
Columbus, OH 43218-0269
1-888-876-3809

Note: Don't forget to consider special interest magazines like *Cobblestone: American History for Kids, Sports Illustrated for*

Kids, National Geographic World, and *Ranger Rick,* all of which can be found in most libraries and magazine racks.

INTERNET RESOURCES

Government Websites for Parents:

www.ed.gov/pubs/parents.html—U.S. Department of Education information including a series of pamphlets called Helping Your Child, with other reports on helping children read, and preparing for college.

www.negp.gov/index.htm—National Educational Goals reports and early childhood information.

Children's Writing Resources—Please see the boxed section in our chapter The Bond Between Reading and Writing, p. 52.

Classic Books and Literature Online—See our mention of the Jolly Roger on-line library of classic children's books in Mixing Books With Other Media, p.75.
(jollyroger.com/treasureisland.html)

Bibliography/
Recommended Reading

Beales, Donna. "Lords of the Library." *School Library Journal* May 1997: 65.

Begley, Sharon. "How to Build a Baby's Brain." *Newsweek* Special Issue Spring/Summer 1997: 28-32.

Berryhill, Allison. "Raising a Reader." *Better Homes and Gardens* Aug. 1997: 62-65.

"Books Every Child Should Read: A Western Canon, Jr." Internet, HomeArts network: Hearst Communications, 1998. (http://homearts.com/depts/relat/bookintr.htm)

Burns, Mary M. and Ann A. Flowers. "Have Book Bag, Will Travel: A Practical Guide to Reading Aloud." *The Horn Book Magazine* March/April 1997: 182 -189.

Butler, Dorothy. *Babies Need Books*. New York: Atheneum, 1980.

(Supports reading and introducing books from babyhood. Includes a treasure trove of book suggestions and approach methods.)

—————. *Cushla and Her Books*. Boston: Horn Book, 1980.

(This book is based on the case study of a severely handicapped child whose life was transformed by books. It's "must" reading for those who want further evidence of the amazing power of books.)

Calkins, Lucy, and Lydia Bellino. *Raising Lifelong Learners: A Parent's Guide*. Reading, Mass.: Addison-Wesley, 1997.

(Thoughtful approaches and personal testimony on promoting literacy in the home and at school, both with regard to reading and writing.)

Eyre, Frank. *British Children's Books in the Twentieth Century*. New York: Dutton, 1973.

Fox, Barbara J. and Maripat Wright. "Connecting school and home literacy experiences through cross-age reading." *The Reading Teacher* 50 (1997): 396-402.

Fulghum, Robert. *All I Ever Really Need to Know I Learned in Kindergarten: Uncommon Thoughts on Common Things*. New York: Villard, 1988.

Gralla, Preston. *Online Kids: A Young Surfer's Guide to Cyberspace*. New York: John Wiley & Sons, 1996.

International Reading Association, Children's Literature and Reading Special Interest Group. "1996 Notable Books for a Global Society." *The Reading Teacher* 50 (1997): 476-481.

Karl, Jean. *From Childhood to Childhood: Children's Books and Their Creators*. New York: John Day, 1971.

(Well-known children's book editor Jean Karl's reflections on the realm of children's literature as well as the nuts and bolts of what goes into the production of a good book, from the writer's mind to the printing presses.)

Keeshan, Robert. *Books To Grow By: Fun Children's Books Recommended by Bob Keeshan, TV's Captain Kangaroo*. Minneapolis: Fairview Press, 1996.

(For years Keeshan advocated children's books as the popular main character in the beloved morning children's program, *Captain Kangaroo*. This book lists his favorites for children up to age eight.)

Kennedy, Maxwell T. ed. *Make Gentle the Life of This World: The Vision of Robert F. Kennedy*. New York: Harcourt Brace, 1998.

Kingman, Lee. ed. *Newbery and Caldecott Medal Books: 1956-1965*. Boston: Horn Book, 1965.

————. *Newbery and Caldecott Medal Books: 1966-1975.* Boston: Horn Book, 1975.

————. *Newbery and Caldecott Medal Books: 1976-1985.* Boston: Horn Book, 1986.

Kropp, Paul. *Raising a Reader: Make Your Child a Reader for Life.* New York: Doubleday-Main Street Books, 1996.

(Offers good information about reading programs in schools, as well as ideas on how to entice reluctant readers. Juicy tidbits in the margins make for fun reading.)

Laliberte, Richard. "How to Nurture a Love of Reading and Writing." *Good Housekeeping* Oct. 1996: 162-164.

Lancia, Peter J. "Literary Borrowing: The effects of literature on children's writing." *The Reading Teacher* 50 (1997): 470-475.

Landsberg, Michele. *Reading for the Love Of It/Best Books for Young Readers.* New York: Prentice Hall, 1987.

Lanes, Selma G. *Down the Rabbit Hole: Adventures and Misadventures in the Realm of Children's Literature.* New York: Atheneum, 1976.

(Sound criticism and insights into the world of children's literature. Published in the 1970s, this book is dated in some parts, but it's plenty relevant in most areas.)

Leonhardt, Mary. *Parents Who Love Reading, Kids Who Don't: How it Happens and What You Can Do About It.* New York: Crown, 1993.

(This book deals directly with issues concerning reluctant readers. Because approaching these children with books is tricky, you'll see here more references to mass-market "hits" like those penned by Stephen King and Danielle Steel.)

Lewis, C.S. *Surprised by Joy: The Shape of My Early Life.* Orlando: Harcourt Brace Jovanovich, 1955.

Liggett, Twila C. and Cynthia Mayer. *The Reading Rainbow Guide to Children's Books: The 101 Best Titles.* New York: Carol Publishing Group, 1994.

(This good reference guide handily groups by categories such as history, emotions, multicultural, and science and nature.)

Lindskoog, John and Kathryn. *How to Grow a Young Reader—A Parent's Guide to Books for Kids.* Wheaton, Illinois: Harold Shaw, 1989.

(Includes lists such as "30 of the Best Books from the Past for Children Today," plus information about where to order copies of eighteenth-century classics.)

Lipson, Eden Ross. *The New York Times Parent's Guide to the Best Books for Children*. New York: Random House, 1988.

(A sound, easy reference book list by the *Times'* children's book editor, with just enough information about each book to spark ideas, and multiple cross-reference index lists including by subject and "read-aloud" potential.)

Moeller, Babette, and Naomi Hupert. "Reading in the Age of Multimedia." *Electronic Learning* May/June 1997: 54.

Nespeca, Sue McLeaf. "Literacy Begins at Home: 25 Ways to Make Sure Reading Runs in the Family." *School Library Journal* May 1996: 26-29.

Paterson, Katherine. *Gates of Excellence: On Reading and Writing Books for Children*. New York: Dutton, 1988.

(A collection of essays by Newbery award winning writer Katherine Paterson, which plumb Paterson's interesting childhood and experiences as a writer and mother of four.)

Schmitz, Terri. " 'Tell the Lady What You Like': Shopping for Children's Books." *The Horn Book Magazine* March/April 1997: 171-177.

Seuling, Barbara. *How to Write a Children's Book and Get It Published*. New York: Charles Scribner's Sons, 1991.

Soundy, Cathleen S. "Nurturing Literacy with Infants and Toddlers in Group Settings." *Childhood Education* Spring 1997: 149–153.

Trelease, Jim. *The New Read-Aloud Handbook*. Revised edition. New York: Penguin, 1989. (A must for a parent's own Magic Bookshelf.)

Index

Notes

Tell us what you think

The authors of this book want to hear your ideas for future editions of this book as well as suggestions for other information resources that could help make your family stronger. Please take a few minutes to jot down your own experiences, the titles of books that have been winners among your own children, or questions you would like to have answered. Also, we want to know what you think could be improved in this book. Help us make it an even better value for parents, or others who want to help special children move into the world of great literature. Thank you.

_____
_____
_____
_____
_____
_____
_____
_____
_____
_____
_____
_____
_____

Please send your suggestions to:
Janie and Richard Jarvis
c/o Lorica Publishing
PO Box 53303
Atlanta, Ga. 30355
e-mail: loricapub@excite.com

Buy this book

Perhaps you're reading this book in the library or borrowed a copy from a friend. Or, maybe you know others who need help building Magic Bookshelves in their own homes. If you've enjoyed this book, think what a great gift it would be to help another family start creating their own magic by reading good books and starting a collection. To order, just mail this form (or a copy) to the address below. Feel free to call us at (404) 702-8620 with any questions.

__ Yes, send me ___ copies of *The Magic Bookshelf* right away at $16.95 each. Add $3 for shipping on the first book and $2 for each additional book. (Please include sales tax in Georgia.) My address is below. I understand that I may return any books for a full refund—for any reason, no questions asked.

Name _____

Address _____

City/State/Zip _____

E-mail _____

Phone (Optional) _____

I've enclosed a check or money order for $_____

__ No, I don't want to order at this time, but I would like to be on Lorica Publishing's mailing list for information on future releases.

Please mail your order to:
Lorica Publishing
PO Box 53303
Atlanta, Ga. 30355

For information on bulk orders and quantity discounts, please call (404) 702-8620. Send e-mail information requests to: loricapub@excite.com